# WHAT'S YOURS IS MINE

# WHAT'S YOURS IS MINE

## Open Access and the Rise of Infrastructure Socialism

•

**ADAM THIERER**
**CLYDE WAYNE CREWS JR.**

CATO
INSTITUTE
Washington, D.C.

**Library of Congress Cataloging-in-Publication Data**

Thierer, Adam D.
  What's yours is mine : open access and the rise of infrastructure
socialism / Adam Thierer, Clyde Wayne Crews.
      p. cm.
  Includes bibliographical references and index.
  ISBN 1-930865-42-2 (pbk. : alk. paper)
    1. Public utilities—Law and legislation—United States. 2. Infrastructure
(Economics)—United States.   3. Monopolies—United States.
4. Competition, Unfair—United States.   5. Law and economics—
United States.   I. Crews, Clyde Wayne.   II. Title.

KF2094.6.T48 2003
384'.041'0973--dc21                                                    2003043782


Cover design by Elise Rivera.
Printed in the United States of America.

CATO INSTITUTE
1000 Massachusetts Ave., N.W.
Washington, D.C. 20001
www.cato.org

# Contents

# Introduction

Should owners or their rivals get to call the shots with respect to access to networks and technologies? An increasing amount of legislative and regulatory activity in America today is concerned with securing mandatory "open access" to high-tech sector networks and services. Open-access regulations require that a company or industry sector share its network, facilities, or specific technologies with rival companies so that those competitors may enjoy the same access to the array of citizens or potential consumers as does the incumbent.

Open-access regulation is spreading from one industry sector to another and is quickly coming to be viewed by legislators and bureaucrats alike as the default regulatory regime for network-related technologies and industries. Seemingly every network-related industry or technology—electricity, railroads, phone companies, cable companies, wireless carriers, eBay's auction listings, AOL Time Warner's instant messaging service, the Visa/Mastercard network, Microsoft's Windows operating system, and even the Google search engine—has at some point been the target of those who support open-access regulation.

The faith in open access to networks, however, is based on a flawed assumption: that such access represents a limited, competition-enhancing regulatory response to some perceived market failure. In reality, open-access regulation invites a significant expansion in the role government planning plays in markets. It is coercive and, ultimately, isn't meant to be temporary by many public officials and organizations that are its proponents. Open-access policies necessarily impose a burdensome regime of price and quality controls and attendant regulation, and usher in litigation. Rather than create competitive market rivalry, open access discourages genuine competition and innovation.

The ideas lurking behind calls for forced access to high technology services are among the most perilous regulatory impulses facing

1

America's highly networked economy. While portrayed as a benign, pro-consumer, competition-enhancing intervention, open access is in reality *forced sharing*, not competition. As a regulatory edict requiring private companies to surrender control over the systems or technologies they have developed to others who haven't developed such systems of their own, it has the explicit goal of forcing involuntary trade across what ought to be privately controlled property. The forced-access virus continues to spread even as the pages of the business press overflow with tales of the anguish and regulatory mire this allegedly competitive model has visited on targeted industries.

### Property Rights vs. Parasitism

To create and preserve the best preconditions for wealth creation and innovation in the economy, it is more sensible to regard networks as private property rather than public-utility-like vessels that should be subject to common carrier–style regulations. Unfortunately, those lobbying for open access, whatever the industry sector, want to hitch an uninvited ride on another's property rather than construct their own or make a voluntary business deal for access. That impulse is incompatible with the aims of the network owner, and incompatible with the emergence of future networks. There can be no stable regulatory resolutions of such fundamental cross-purposes.

Continued embrace of access regulation threatens to turn Internet and other network-related businesses into lazy public utilities, neutralizing the natural competitive impulse of firms to devise alternative business models and rival networks capable of displacing an entrenched incumbent. Consider reform of telecommunications and electricity, where the expressed goal has been creating competition and better customer service. Under genuine competition, regulators would disappear. In contrast, the imposition of mandatory access would armor-plate regulators at an arguably critical moment in business history when a number of affected network companies should instead be creating the redundancy and overlap necessary to better serve tomorrow's customers. Mandatory access policies, the administration of which necessitates technocratic central management, compromise entrepreneurial incentives to embrace innovations. These policies also harm service reliability because improvements and dependability rely on regulators rather than competitors making the key moves.

While contracts between firms for voluntary access are clearly desirable and, as will be seen, to be expected as a result of market pressures, imposing access artificially sacrifices network and technological advances. Where nonowners get to determine the terms of service for rivals' preexisting networks and technologies, future iterations of those services will be delayed or won't emerge at all.

### The Many Faces of Forced Access

Forced-access appeals take different forms. Some advocates explicitly seek access to an incumbent's physical network, as seen in the attempts by newer classes of electric power generators to secure access to competitors' electric wires.[1] The case study of electricity markets contained in Chapter 5 details this attempted expropriation of the electricity grid by rivals.

Another example, discussed in Chapter 7, is America Online's pursuit of access to AT&T's cable networks, a crusade AOL abandoned when it became a significant cable infrastructure owner on its merger with Time Warner.[2] A much older example of forced access in action comes from the video programming marketplace where "must-carry" mandates have required that cable (and later satellite) network owners provide space on their systems to rival local broadcast television stations that have successfully petitioned policymakers for a free ride on rival distribution networks. Chapter 8 reviews the history of must-carry regulation.

In other instances, a petitioner may hope to accomplish the same end—access to the product of another's effort—via "structural separation" of integrated components of an incumbent's business that effectively revoke that owner's proprietary interest in his property. A key example of this approach is the proposal to split Baby Bell telephone companies into "wholesale" and "retail" operations.[3] The aim of this policy would be to forcibly alter the incentives of those companies by dampening the inclination to discriminate against competitors' traffic (taking for granted that doing so is a good thing).[4] Chapter 6 offers an in-depth exploration of forced-access regulation of the local telephone marketplace, which has been the most comprehensive experiment in open-access regulation to date.

Finally, as Chapter 9 argues, the proposed breakup of Microsoft into separate operating system and applications companies is a variant of this philosophy of altering a business structure to change incentives. The intent of that original June 7, 2000, order by Judge Thomas Penfield Jackson in the D.C. District Court, since overturned, was to remove Microsoft's incentives to feature its own software offerings over those of rivals (again taking for granted that doing so is a good thing for technology, competition, consumers, and capitalism).[5] This approach to software competition has now carried over into instant messaging.

### Forced Access Means Mutant Markets

From the perspective of free markets and laissez faire capitalism, open-access schemes create mutant entities, contrived "businesses" or industries that did not and never would have emerged by way of actual competitive market processes—*and that therefore have no proper role to play in the voluntary competitive marketplace.* They are artificial creations, the spawn of special-interest pleadings rather than market processes, designed to eliminate the requirement that rivals either broker voluntary access deals or successfully develop competing facilities-based infrastructure. For example, as the discussion of telecommunications policy in Chapter 6 outlines in detail, extensive forced-access regulation of the local telephone exchange gave rise to a substantial but temporary expansion of small access resellers who could not have existed without the assistance of Federal Communications Commission bureaucrats. And despite the tireless efforts of regulators to preserve such artificial market entry through aggressive network-sharing mandates on incumbent telephone companies, the FCC still could not save such mutant entities from an eventual market downturn.

Open-access mandates overrule market processes by jettisoning the principles of private property and voluntary exchange—even though those principles form the bedrock on which future waves of network expansion and progress depend. The "essential provider" vision that the open-access model both accepts and imposes should be rejected in favor of a new principle: *competition in the creation of networks is as important as competition in the goods and services that get sold over new or existing networks.* Property rights in "long and thin" assets like networks should be respected, just as we recognize property rights in "short and fat" assets like houses, cars, and television sets.

## Competition Comes in Many Forms

The same incentives that underlie self-serving calls for antitrust action against an efficient rival underlie calls for open access to a rival's property. Competitors motivated by such antitrust activism will be unlikely to acknowledge that the dominance of a rival represents legitimate competition, or at least the outcome of such competition. Competition takes many forms; it should be understood as existing both *within* and *across* industry sectors. For example, with respect to cable modem Internet service, not only can Internet service providers (ISPs) negotiate access to cable lines—representing competition within the cable modem industry—but the cable industry isn't the only one providing broadband, or high-speed, Internet. That opens the field to additional initiatives by ISPs or other entrepreneurs. For example, broadband is expanding via digital subscriber line (DSL), land-based wireless options, and satellite. And, of course, the dial-up Internet access that the vast majority of Web surfers still use provides the competitive backdrop and remains adequate for the needs of millions. Different players are active in each subsector, all seeking the same customers, providing checks and balances for the entire competitive system regardless of any (likely temporary) dominance that may occur within any one subsector.

The forced interconnection paradigm should not be imposed on broadband data networks or instant messaging, nor should it be used to restructure great mainline network industries like electricity. Incumbents naturally resist opening their networks for below cost or for unacceptable terms, and mandating that they do so is not desirable from the standpoint of market evolution. Private business decisions can only be overruled though force, creating nonmarket entities not equipped to deal with technological change and market demands. The inefficiencies and consumer harms created by government regulation and interference with network access policies and growth will outweigh the *potential* but unlikely abuses by private network owners that allegedly justify demands for access. While it goes against the grain of policymaking sentiments today, more substantial competition in networks can emerge if policymakers stop trying to mandate it. A better philosophical and principled approach is to assure that regulation does not stand in the way of network duplication. For example, policymakers could eliminate artificial, government-created barriers to genuine competition like electricity franchises that outlaw competition against the incumbent.

The answers to questions regarding the shape of tomorrow's network industries are not simply to be gleaned from today's conditions and set forth for the ages in assorted bureaucracies' regulatory decrees. Information about the proper structure of myriad networks will be created by shifting market conditions every day. Appropriate market structures today will perhaps not be appropriate in 2, 5, or 10 years. But the natural and necessary process that makes the needed changes cannot occur if industries succumb to open-access disease. Markets must be allowed to work. Policymakers must not look at snapshots of the market, they must look at underlying market processes. In that vein, this book sets forth the case against the infrastructure socialism inherent in forced-access schemes and urges policymakers to embrace the evolutionary nature of the free market.

PART I:

OPEN ACCESS: THEORY AND REALITY

# 1. The Case against Forced Access

Despite its advocacy by regulators, misguided consumer advocates, and opportunistic businesspeople, forced-access regulation has many problems.

### Problem 1: Forced Access Is a Taking of Private Property

Forced-access regulation is essentially at war with private property rights. In one sense, forced-access regulation is really nothing more than a variant of socialism since it demands that private companies surrender control of their systems or technologies to a governmental vision of efficient and proper distribution of resources.

Forced-access crusades are always undertaken in the name of advancing consumer choice, competition, and "openness."[1] But even if forced access helped advance these ends, the ends do not justify the means. Free market competition means that private property owners—even owners of network properties—are at liberty to use their property as they see fit, and citizens are free to shop around for better arrangements when they feel they are not getting the best deal possible. The alternative is that of government bureaucrats demanding that control over private property be surrendered. Commenting on open-access conditions imposed on the AOL Time Warner merger, American Enterprise Institute scholar James K. Glassman noted that regulators "have served notice to high-tech firms that if they make big investments in new products like cable modems and instant messaging services, their property rights to those innovations may be stripped from them at will for political reasons."[2]

Moreover, because forced-access regulation forces private property owners to surrender the ownership or control of their property to regulators, there remains a legitimate question of whether it represents an unconstitutional taking under the Fifth Amendment to the Constitution. Some scholars, such as J. Gregory Sidak of the American Enterprise Institute and Daniel F. Spulber of the Northwestern University Graduate School of Management, argue that this is the case even for industries that were formerly treated as regulated monopolies, such as electricity and local telecommunications. They argue that these entities deserve compensation for the past investments or "stranded costs" they have incurred in the past.[3]

> The facilities of the regulated network industries did not fall like manna from heaven, but rather were established by incumbent utilities through the expenditures of their investors. Utilities made past expenditures to perform obligations to serve in expectation of the reasonable opportunity to recover the costs of investment plus a competitive rate of return. Investors must be compensated for those past costs; it follows a fortiori that investors must be offered additional compensation if existing responsibilities are perpetuated or new burdens imposed.[4]

Stranded cost recovery remains a controversial proposition given that these entities enjoyed geographic service monopolies and guaranteed rates of return.[5] But while these sectors do not necessarily deserve any special consideration or compensation for the investments they made decades ago, what should not be the least bit controversial is the proposition that these entities deserve to be compensated for future takings of their property in a deregulated marketplace in which they have lost their monopolistic service territories and guaranteed rates of return.

Consequently, if forced-access mandates are being applied to such network industries in an attempt to transition them into a more competitive marketplace, they will need to be compensated for the costs they and their investors are now incurring as they deploy new systems and technologies. Regulators cannot continue to confiscate network assets without just compensation merely because certain portions of those networks may have been deployed years ago. Of course, as discussed below, the better solution is to end all exclusive service territories and regulatory advantages for these entities and comprehensively deregulate these markets immediately to avoid such takings controversies in the future. If forced-access mandates are not applied, of course, there would be no takings concern to begin with.

It has also been alleged that a regulatory taking might occur when "must-carry" rules are imposed on cable and satellite companies. Such regulations require those companies to carry the signals of broadcast television stations without compensation. Must-carry mandates were imposed on the cable industry through the Cable Television Consumer Protection and Competition Act of 1992 and on the satellite industry through the Satellite Home Viewer Improvement Act of 1999. The rules compel firms to carry broadcast television signals on their networks without receiving compensation for doing so.

"Must-carry rules constitute a taking of property," argues Harvard Law School constitutional scholar Laurence H. Tribe. "Must-carry rules do not simply regulate the manner in which cable operators use their systems. Rather, they effectively condemn a portion of cable operators' property and *turn it over to third parties* who are entitled to exclusive use of the channels in question on a continuing basis. This system is effectively the exercise of eminent domain power over a portion of the cable system."[6] Roger Pilon, vice president of legal affairs at the Cato Institute, has noted that, "Under must carry ... we have in essence a publicly sanctioned private condemnation, with local broadcasters 'taking' the channels that belong to cable operators. And as is the case with so many modern regulatory takings, the cable operators are made to serve the public—and made to serve their broadcast competitors, in particular—while bearing the whole cost themselves."[7]

The courts have on occasion supported the notion that mandatory access to network properties can constitute a taking. In the 1994 case of *Bell Atlantic Corp. v. FCC*, the D.C. Circuit court struck down the FCC's physical collocation rules, which gave competitors access to the central offices owned by local telephone companies. The court found the FCC collocation rules to be a violation of the Fifth Amendment since a "permanent physical occupation authorized by government is a taking without regard to the public interest that it may serve."[8] Likewise, in the 1982 case *Loretto v. Teleprompter Manhattan CATV Corp.*, the Supreme Court dealt with state regulations requiring building owners to grant access to cable firms for purposes of wiring and attachments. The Court held that even a "minor but permanent physical occupation of an owner's property authorized by government constitutes a taking of property for which just compensation is due."[9] So certainly a strong claim can be made by property owners that mandatory network access imposes costs and burdens on them that must be taken into account by policymakers.

At a minimum, just compensation is due for such takings, but the better policy would be for policymakers to reject confiscatory infrastructure-sharing mandates altogether since they are at odds not merely with private property rights but even with the stated aim of open-access supporters—that of better service to consumers.

### Problem 2: Forced Access Hinders Innovation and Network Integrity

Forced-access regulation rejects the long-standing and time-tested proprietary model of business ownership and management. Companies create goods, services, technologies, and networks in the hope of maximizing shareholder wealth. Often, if companies hope to generate profits on those investments, they must tightly control access to their product to ensure they can recoup their initial investment. "In an efficient economic system, risk and reward go together," notes David Kopel of the Heartland Institute. "Whoever takes the risk of failure should reap the reward of success. If a company must bear all the risks, but must share much of the rewards with its competitors, the company will stop taking risks."[10] And Daniel F. Spulber and Christopher S. Yoo, associate professor of law at Vanderbilt University Law School, argue that "regulation that compels access to networks at regulated prices that fall below market rates in effect requires network owners to subsidize competitors."[11]

For example, automakers would not produce new lines of cars if they were forced to share the vehicle design plans, or specific component innovations, with their competitors. Forced-access regulation, however, presumes that new products, systems, or technologies will be produced by companies regardless of the regulatory environment or legal incentives in place. But firms will not develop and deploy expensive new goods and services if the regulatory regime requires that they share the fruits of their investment and innovation. This is especially true for network industries where elaborate and expensive systems of wires, switching services, support systems, and other technologies must already be in place before one can hope to attract customers and generate a return on investment. A prerequisite that network providers share these facilities can, therefore, chill overall investment incentives. As AT&T chairman and CEO Michael Armstrong put it in 1998, "No company will invest billions of dollars to become a facilities-based broadband

12

service provider if competitors who have not invested a penny of capital nor taken an ounce of risk can come along and get a free ride on the investments and risks of others."[12]

The impact of access regulation on infrastructure integrity must also be considered. At a time when many express concern over network security and critical infrastructure protection, this concern is particularly pertinent. One of the core fundamentals of security is redundancy. For example, in contrast to the dedicated-line telephone system, the Internet was designed to withstand physical damage by routing traffic (via packet-switching) around any disruption. John C. Wohlstetter of the Discovery Institute has pointed out that the telecommunications vulnerabilities exposed on September 11 could be attributable to "current telecommunications regulatory policies that prefer shared local exchange facilities to separate ones, thus discouraging multiple local facilities."[13]

### Problem 3: Forced Access Discourages Entrepreneurial Competition from Rivals

Not only does forced-access regulation discourage investment and innovation by the incumbent network owner, but it also destroys the incentive for rivals to invest in new facilities of their own. In other words, contrived competition via forced access destroys actual competition.

The competition of which forced-access supporters speak is a fiction based on the sharing of existing facilities. Sharing is not competing. When regulators allow one set of companies to engage in regulatory arbitrage by picking and choosing the networks or network components to which they seek access, "it cannot but have a fatally discouraging effect on their own imitative and innovative efforts," says noted regulatory economist Alfred E. Kahn, former head of the now defunct U.S. Civil Aeronautics Board and author of *The Economics of Regulation* and *Letting Go: Deregulating the Process of Deregulation*. Kahn, discussing telecommunications regulation, continues: "When every applicant can be a free rider, at such minimum prices, who is going to build the vehicle? The [Federal Communications] Commission appears completely to have ignored the discouraging effect of their rules on facilities-based competition."[14]

What is true for telecommunications regulation would be equally true in any other industry where interconnection, unbundling, and infrastructure sharing rules are applied haphazardly. Imagine this hypothetical scenario: Lawmakers encourage a large number of firms to enter the market for cola beverages by mandating that Coke and Pepsi share their soda formulas and manufacturing facilities with rival firms at a regulated wholesale rate. New firms are given the right to purchase soda for 17 to 25 percent less than what it actually costs Coke and Pepsi to produce each can or bottle. Having received the products from Coke and Pepsi at such a steeply discounted rate, these new "rivals" then turn around and sell the beverages under their own brand name for a profit.

As a result, several dozen new "competitors" enter a market in which there are currently only two primary providers. Wouldn't this represent a "pro-competitive" result? No, it would not, because it would not promote genuine competitive rivalry to Coke and Pepsi but would instead encourage a handful of opportunists to make money off an existing product without offering the public anything legitimately innovative or unique. Even worse, it might discourage Coke and Pepsi from creating new products, since they would likely fear additional government mandates forcing them to share their innovations with other companies. Finally, while the overall number of firms in the market would increase temporarily, the charade would end once investors realized there was no legitimate business model behind this parasitic regulatory scheme. Even with the generous assistance of bureaucrats, such a regulatory house of cards is bound to collapse if the firms benefiting from it are doing little or nothing to deploy innovative services of their own.

But that scenario illustrates what has happened in the American telecom marketplace in the wake of the implementation of the Telecommunications Act of 1996. Firms are engaging in a blatant form of regulatory arbitrage by reselling access to existing lines to which the government gave them access at generously discounted wholesale rates, which are significantly lower than the likely cost of providing those expensive networks. Under the Telecom Act, such infrastructure socialism was to be limited to the old voice-based copper lines that the Bells already had in the ground for many years while they were still protected monopolies. But the open-ended language and ill-defined terminology of the Telecom Act encouraged creative and quite expansive interpretations of "access" from the start. This led to proposals to apply forced-access mandates elsewhere, such as cable broadband markets, AOL's instant messaging service, and even wireless networks.

Policymakers would be wise to heed the words of Supreme Court Justice Stephen Breyer, who, in the 1999 case of *AT&T Corporation et al. v. Iowa Utilities Board*, warned of the hazards of carrying forced access to extremes: "A totally unbundled world—a world in which competitors share every part of an incumbent's existing system, including, say, billing, advertising, sales staff, and work force (and in which regulators set all unbundling charges)—is a world in which competitors would have little, if anything, to compete about."[15]

### Problem 4: Forced-Access Proponents Often Assume Technological Stasis and Unchanging Marketplace Conditions

The zero-sum mentality that motivates proponents of open access often assumes that once a network has been built and used by a large enough group of consumers, it is the only facility the public can expect to provide service in the future. Somehow, when a company and its shareholders make the expensive investments necessary to provide an innovative new network service, it is a one-time event, never to be repeated. Many forced-access proponents are quick to label some industries "natural monopolies," or certain networks "essential facilities," and then demand companies surrender control over their property to policymakers who will ascertain what is in the public interest.

But is such technological pessimism truly warranted? History suggests the opposite is the case. Ours is an innovative culture and new technologies and industry sectors have developed in the past, and will be developed in the future, but only if creators (1) believe they can reap the fruits of their labor and (2) are not directly or indirectly prohibited by government from entering new markets or providing new services.

Still, skeptics will claim that the fixed costs associated with network development and deployment are substantial, so much so that it is foolish to assume rivals will rise up to offer truly competitive alternatives. The best we can hope for once a network has been built is for its owners to share those facilities with other rivals. Genuine facilities-based competition is assumed to be an impossibility given the prohibitively expensive upfront costs of offering service.

15

The fundamental problem with this theory is that it has been accepted as a self-fulfilling prophecy and not truly tested in the marketplace. By presuming that this theory is an indisputable truth and then preemptively foreclosing market entry in the past, or encouraging unnatural forms of entry in the present, policymakers have in essence not been willing to test the validity of natural monopoly theory. Simply stated, markets have not really been given a chance—or, worse yet, were given a chance, succeeded, and were overruled by policymakers anyway.

### Problem 5: Forced Access Is Increasingly Used as an Anti-Competitive Tool

Burdensome regulation is often advocated by firms who want to shackle their competitors. But using forced-access regulation to beat down rivals can backfire on the firms that seek it.

Before Internet giant America Online's proposed merger with cable and media colossus Time Warner, AOL championed forced-access requirements for cable providers as a way of assuring an audience for its content. AOL, like many other ISPs, feared that in the absence of a forced-access requirement, cable companies would restrict access to their systems or craft exclusive deals with favored ISPs. After the AOL–Time Warner marriage proposal, however, AOL quickly changed its tune to favor *voluntary* open access freely negotiated between carriers and Internet companies.[16]

But rival ISPs and many other companies successfully demanded that federal regulators require the new AOL Time Warner to allow access to their services.[17] As Elizabeth Wasserman of *The Industry Standard* noted at the time, "From Disney to EarthLink to Bell South, an all-star list of enemies has come together to fight the merger of AOL and Time Warner."[18] In addition, AOL was required to open advanced instant messaging services to rivals. The AOL episode illustrates how, if the machinery of government is made available to competitors, they will use it to hamper market leaders. This behavior sends a message to entrepreneurs: the more successful one is and the more customers one attracts, the more likely one will attract rivals seeking regulated access to those same customers.

### Problem 6: Forced Access Necessitates Price Controls and Government Management

Many champions of forced access regard it as a welcome alternative to command-and-control regulatory schemes and regimes of the past. In fact, some supporters claim that forced access is actually deregulatory in character since its long-run objective is a more competitive industry structure—a highly dubious claim and one that is contradicted by recent experience with forced-access regulation.

The debate over forced access typically centers around *what* is being opened and *how* access should be guaranteed. But as complicated and significant as those two questions are, they do not represent the most important issue involved in mandating access to a network or technology. Rather, the most important questions involved in the process are: *At what price* is network access set and *Who sets this price*? As P. H. Longstaff summarizes, "The price charged for access to a company's infrastructure can be the most controversial part of these public policies, and government is usually forced to act as a referee in deciding on a price that is 'fair'...."[19]

In a free market, most firms will grant rivals' access to their proprietary systems or technologies, but they will attempt to strike mutually agreeable terms that will help them amortize their sunk costs and achieve profitability. Forced-access regulation suspends this voluntary negotiating process and substitutes a convoluted price control regime run by bureaucrats. An example is the complex transmission system operation established in California on the restructuring (not deregulation) of its electricity industry.[20] Regulators, rather than market interactions, are then responsible for gauging supply and demand and determining what represents fair compensation for access to a firm's network or technologies.

The regulatory process of establishing such price controls is extremely complex and time-consuming because of its litigious and bureaucratic nature. This, in turn, further delays innovation and investment. "Hands Off the Internet Coalition" president Christopher Wolf argues:

> First, to establish "fair" prices, officials will need to analyze difficult cost allocation issues, write nondiscrimination policies, divide the network into specific elements, and then price each. Expect to see hordes of economists, technical experts and lawyers—especially the lawyers!—weigh in. They will represent everyone with an interest at stake, including the cable company, the phone company, and probably a half-dozen Internet providers. Of course, it won't stop there. Regulators will need to hire their own lawyers, experts, and economists to decide who's correct and what the best public policy would be.[21]

Absent a miracle, the pricing that results from such a process is bound to be inefficient. Lawrence Gasman, president of Communications Industry Researchers, has noted (with respect to FCC mandated interconnection prices, but also generally): "Bureaucrats or even entrepreneurs cannot predict the market price of a product. Thus, absent sheer luck, the FCC mandate either underprices or overprices the service component of the existing networks."[22] Brookings Institution economist Robert Crandall argues that "Flipping a coin is certainly in the set of alternatives to a rate-of-return or cost-based proceedings."[23]

A key case on access pricing was recently handed down by the Supreme Court in the May 2002 decision on *Verizon Communications v. Federal Communications Commission*.[24] Regrettably, the Court upheld the FCC's controversial pricing methodology for access to local phone networks. Interest groups argued that the FCC needed to prevail in that case so that price regulation would continue to guarantee resellers low-cost access to elements of the local telephone network owned by incumbent regional Bell operating companies (RBOCs) or "Baby Bells." Baby Bell rivals argue that such strict price controls are needed because higher prices would remove rivals' incentive to compete with the local phone companies. In terms of genuine facilities-based competition, however, the reverse is true: Higher prices should signal a profit opportunity for entrepreneurs to enter the market and offer services of their own. Again, infrastructure sharing is not true competition.

Unfortunately, yet another recent pricing case upheld the role of regulatory price setting. The Supreme Court in January 2002 ruled that the federal government could regulate the fees that utilities charge to cable companies for attaching broadband services to their poles. The 11th Circuit had ruled earlier that the FCC could not limit rates for such pole sharing.[25] Although FCC Chairman Michael Powell commented, "It is important that the court rejected an interpretation of the Communications Act that could have raised the rates that consumers pay for high-speed Internet access services and derailed the broadband revolution,"[26] the reverse could be true. Because rates for attachments for traditional video would not have been affected by the decision, monthly rates might have risen only about $1.50.[27] That amount hardly seems overwhelming, and keeping rates down $18 a year hardly seems worth enshrining the principle of regulated rates and sacrificing market pricing. The better solution would be to privatize the poles or auction to the cable companies rights the poles and let the market sort out the optimal price of interconnection.

Finally, forced-access regimes require significant increases in regulatory spending and staffing to enforce their price controls. This is perhaps best exemplified by FCC efforts to determine the "fair" price of access to the local telephone network.[28] FCC spending and staffing levels have risen significantly in recent years despite the supposedly deregulatory thrust of the Telecommunications Act of 1996.

For example, from 1997 until March 1999, the FCC promulgated 497 final rules. That is almost the combined total number of rules promulgated by the Department of Defense (165), the Veterans Administration (81), the Department of State (42), the Department of Justice (133), and the Department of Education (133) during the same period. In fiscal year 1998, no other federal agency produced as many "major" rules—defined under the Congressional Review Act of 1996 as rules that result in an impact on the economy of more than $100 million—as did the FCC, which published 27 percent of all federal agency major rules during that fiscal year.[29]

Greg Sidak of the American Enterprise Institute also notes that FCC spending has risen by 37 percent since the mid-90s and the number of pages in the *FCC Record*—the official compendium of all FCC rulemakings—has nearly tripled over the same period. Moreover, Sidak found that the number of communications industry lawyers grew by 73 percent between December 1994 and December 1998.[30] Any time a government body proposes that a forced-access regime be applied to a new technology or industry sector, similar expansions in agency spending and bureaucracy can be anticipated.

## Problem 7: Forced Access Is Unnecessary in an Environment of Proliferating Choices

The rise of forced-access proposals comes at a time when Americans have access to an unprecedented array of choices in the markets in question. Consider the communications industry.

Not so long ago, citizens and consumers could more legitimately have lamented living in a world characterized by information scarcity and limited communications and entertainment options. Today, however, the chief complaint of average Americans about communications systems and services is "information overload." Hundreds, if not thousands of television channels, delivered by cable, satellite, and antenna, are available. Internet access to the home via telephone, cable, or satellite is spreading, leading to "digital opportunity" rather than a "digital divide."[31] Computer systems are available for under $400, and a variety of software is at the fingertips of consumers. And the list of choices goes on: videocassette recorders, digital video discs, portable MP3 players, video cameras, pagers, cellular phones, and so on. Competition is even emerging quite rapidly in the broadband network creation business with new wireline and wireless networking options appearing.

Increasingly, choice is emerging within older industries like electric power markets as well. Developments such as distributed generation, better power-flow technologies, microturbines and fuel cells, and extensive backup power capabilities (demanded by technology companies that cannot afford to rely on a regulated, unreliable grid) are all remaking what had been a rather boring utility industry. Likewise, railroads have faced stiff competition from surface and air shippers in the wake of trucking and airline deregulation.

Forced-access regulation does not deserve the credit for the proliferation of services in these markets. These technologies and networks are being made available because companies believed consumers would demand them and be willing to pay for them. The profit motive and the proprietary model of business management are responsible for network innovations, not government access mandates.

### Problem 8: Forced Access Ignores the Real Monopoly Problem—Government-Sanctioned Service Franchises

Forced-access solutions misdiagnose the real monopoly problem in many network industries: government-protected service franchises or territories. In assessing the possibility of network competition, it is important to recognize that artificial, government-created barriers often exist or existed that preclude rivalry or voluntary contracting among providers. Prime examples are cable television and electric power company franchises. Historically, state and municipal governments have legislated exclusive local service territories, deliberately limiting geographic competition to one company per region.

These franchises create a market power problem by foreclosing entry by potential competitors. For example, in the electricity industry, states, public utility commissions, and localities restrain voluntary trade through exclusive franchises that they deem to be in the public interest. The "certificates of convenience and necessity" required to sell electricity in Colorado are typical of artificial market barriers:

> No public utility shall begin the construction of a new facility, plant, or system or of any extension of its facility, plant, or system without first having obtained from the [public utilities] commission a certificate that the present or future public convenience and necessity require or will require such construction.[32]

Any such remaining policies need to be struck from the books. There is no justification for mandating open-access policies in the name of promoting competition when the absence of competition is artificially created by franchise laws in the first place. A worthwhile policy of promoting competition would target these artificial impediments to market entry. Indeed, perhaps the greatest contribution policymakers could make today would be to remove all governmental barriers to competition. To a great extent, the absence of competition requires a concerted governmental effort to sustain it. Competition will happen if it isn't outlawed.

There is a difference between mandated "competition" via open access—and simply allowing competition where it is now prohibited. If competition is the goal, then governments should permit voluntary trade where it is forbidden; but that does not require the additional leap of imposing *involuntary* trade across networks. Open access compounds distortions already created by exclusive franchises. If reformers embrace open access while leaving exclusive service territories intact, they create an industry that deforms as the free elements ooze around the regulated components. Competition should mean the disappearance of the regulator; open access assures that the regulator has to stick around to deal with distortions and complaints.

### Problem 9: Forced-Access Mandates Applied to Communications Systems Raise Serious First Amendment Concerns

In the context of communications policy, forced-access mandates can raise special First Amendment concerns. If the government compels the owner of a communications network to use its property in ways not of its choosing, First Amendment rights come into question. Some argue that corporations do not enjoy the same First Amendment rights as individuals. But a corporation is nothing more than a collection of many individuals (managers, employees, shareholders, etc.) who have First Amendment rights.

For example, the must-carry mandates imposed on cable and satellite companies clearly involve an element of forced speech. In fact, the cable industry has been involved in a protracted legal battle with Congress and the FCC over these rules. These decisions and rulings have been contradictory in nature: some have been decided in favor of network providers' free speech rights and others have sanctioned must-carry mandates. But in the endless back-and-forth legal melee, legislators, regulators, and judges have always recognized the potential threat posed to cable and satellite firms' First Amendment rights. Sadly, however, ambiguous "public interest" goals have often trumped free speech rights with lawmakers and the courts buying into the broadcast sector's argument that access to cable and satellite systems can be compelled in the name of "preserving the benefits of free, over-the-air local television" or "promoting the widespread dissemination of information from a multiplicity of sources."[33]

Despite the court's legal schizophrenia regarding must-carry, a strong case can be made that forcing network owners to provide space on their systems to others abridges speech rights both by forcing them to carry content they might not want to and also by potentially denying them the ability to carry other forms of speech that they find preferable. Forced-access mandates that require owners of broadband networks to open their facilities to third parties likewise raise First Amendment concerns that have yet to be resolved by the courts.

## Conclusion

In summary, forced-access mandates reject property rights, ignore economic incentives, and misunderstand the evolutionary nature of the free market. For these and a host of other reasons, they create more problems than they solve and should be abandoned where currently in place or opposed when debated in the future.

## 2. Debunking "Natural Monopoly" and "Essential Facility" Rationales for Forced-Access Regulation

The most vociferous supporters of forced-access schemes are companies that recognize they can serve their self-interest by petitioning public officials for access to a rival's network. While proponents drape themselves in the cloak of the public interest and claim that access mandates will protect consumers, in reality such pleas represent efforts to skim off their rivals' best customers or undermine efforts by larger companies to serve new customer bases.

A more sophisticated academic defense of forced access, however, is based on the economic doctrines of "natural monopoly" and "essential facility." A marketplace is said to exhibit natural monopoly characteristics when "average costs decline over so large a range of outputs that a single firm would have a big cost advantage over multiple firms serving the same market," according to noted legal scholar and U.S. Court of Appeals for the Seventh Circuit Judge Richard A. Posner.[1] More succinctly, W. Kip Viscusi, John M. Vernon, and Joseph E. Harrington argue, "An industry is a natural monopoly if the production of a particular good or service by a single firm minimizes cost."[2]

The concept of essential facilities is often treated as a derivative of natural monopoly theory, but exact definitions of the term are hard to come by in economic literature. Typically, when scholars or policymakers employ the phrase, they are doing so under the assumption that a given firm's network, technology, or other business system is fundamental to the survival of all other potential competitors in the field and cannot be duplicated by those rivals. Therefore—or so the theory goes—access to that system must be compelled by force of law. Some scholars, such as Glen O. Robinson, have appropriately questioned antitrust law's suspicion of firms' refusals to deal with rivals, arguing that such refusals should not

23

be an antitrust offense except when the concern in question is an essential facility.[3] But what, exactly, is essential? And why should it matter?

## Doctrinal Deficiencies

While they are accepted orthodoxy among many modern economists, the doctrines of essential facility and natural monopoly were not accepted by many classical economists and they remain fundamentally flawed. Their three major deficiencies are discussed below.

### Inherent Ambiguity

The definitions of these doctrines are highly subjective and open-ended in nature. Beginning with natural monopoly theory, it is readily apparent that there is nothing "natural" about a monopoly that government defines and protects. A monopoly indeed exists if the government forecloses all other possible entrants from the marketplace, but there is nothing "natural" about that. These are genuine monopolies—in the correct sense of the term—businesses protected by the coercive powers of government, and they should be dismantled. As Dominick T. Armentano argues, "Government, and not the market, is the source of monopoly power. Government licensing, certificates of public convenience, franchises, tariffs, and other legally restrictive devices can and do create monopoly, and monopoly power, for specific business organizations protected from open competition."[4]

Other economists have challenged the notion that monopolies are in any sense natural. Writing in a 1966 edition of the *Antitrust Bulletin*, James R. Nelson, professor of economics at Amherst College, argued:

> One of the most unfortunate phrases ever introduced into law or economics was the phrase "natural monopoly." Every monopoly is a product of public policy. No present monopoly, public or private, can be traced back through history in a pure form. "Natural monopolies" in fact originated in response to a belief that some goal, or goals, of public policy would be advanced by encouraging or permitting a monopoly to be formed, and discouraging or forbidding future competition with this monopoly.[5]

Nonetheless, many modern economists or politicians have embraced this term to fit their own philosophical agendas or economic assumptions. They have argued that firms that have gained a temporary stronghold in a given marketplace were guilty of being natural monopolies and then imposed a series of entry and operational controls on that sector of the economy. Too often it was abundantly clear that these actions were driven by something other than sound economics. After conducting a comprehensive survey of literature on the subject, Manhattan Institute economist Thomas Hazlett has argued:

> The economists' analysis of the inefficiency of unregulated natural monopoly markets did not spring from a scientific or particularly scholarly research program but in response to "a growing clamor for more government." Indeed many of the early natural monopoly writers had attacked the problem because of personal ideological agendas; their politics preceded their studies.[6]

Similar problems exist with essential facility theory. What exactly qualifies as an essential facility and who is in a position to make such a determination? This is an even more amorphous concept than natural monopoly. Exactly who is omniscient enough to declare a certain facility, technology, or network essential in nature? Was the telegraph an essential facility? The horse-drawn carriage? The steamboat? Google's Internet search engine? Supreme Court cases dealing with essential facilities doctrine have not provided much guidance on the question and have been remarkably ambiguous and open-ended. As antitrust scholar and Harvard University Law School professor Phillip Areeda has noted:

> The [Supreme Court] cases support the doctrine only by implication and in highly qualified ways. You will not find any case that provides a consistent rationale for the doctrine or that explores the social costs and benefits or the administrative costs of requiring the creator of an asset to share it with a rival. It is less a doctrine than epithet, indicating some exception to the right to keep one's creations to oneself, but not telling us what those exceptions are.[7]

A brief review of much of the cases employing this "epithet," as Areeda calls it, makes it equally clear the lengths to which the concept will be contorted by plaintiffs seeking access to someone else's facilities. Areeda notes that essential facilities doctrine has been used to support:

- A rock musician seeking admission to the local auditorium;[8]
- A teletype machine marketer complaining that its competitor will not sell machines for it;[9]
- A ski resort complaining that a rival resort will not engage in joint marketing with it;[10]
- A maker of "muscle building" food supplements demanding that a bodybuilding magazine accept its ads;[11]
- A paper retailer complaining that other paper retailers will not admit it to their wholesale buying co-op;[12]
- An anesthesiologist insisting that the local hospital, using in-house anesthesiologists, allow him to perform anesthesiological services as well;[13]
- A would-be oil seller, who had no storage tanks of his own, demanding to use those of an incumbent seller;[14] and
- A company called Berkey that demanded to know the results of the Kodak Corporation's research before Kodak even marketed its own innovations.[15]

A similar review of the Supreme Court cases dealing with essential facilities theory leads Abbott B. Lipsky Jr., senior competition counsel for the Coca-Cola Company, and J. Gregory Sidak of the American Enterprise Institute to conclude that, "Despite academic criticism, courts have never provided a coherent rationale for the limitations of the doctrine."[16] Lawrence J. White, professor of economics at the New York University Stern School of Business, likewise notes that, "Unfortunately, neither the courts nor Congress has ever clearly specified what constitutes an essential facility for antitrust purposes."[17] And University of Arizona law professor James R. Ratner concurs, noting, "The Supreme Court ... has never provided an appropriate essential facilities analysis."[18]

So it is clear that neither natural monopoly theory nor essential facilities doctrine has been particularly well clarified by the courts or regulatory agencies. Rather, both concepts are based on arbitrary, open-ended interpretations that purport to support the public interest but in reality end up supporting the interests of disgruntled competitors.

### Static View of a Market Economy

The second problem with the concepts of natural monopoly and essential facilities is that they ignore or reject the evolutionary nature of a market economy. They are based on a static view of economics that treats technological progress as fixed or unchanging over time. As P. H. Longstaff has commented, "Discussions of essential facilities often ignore the existence of alternative channels in which the traffic in question could flow."[19] For example, while at one point in time there was only one bridge over the Mississippi River, it did not mean others were not to follow. To make policy under the assumption that no other bridges could be built would be short-sighted. Worse yet, to establish policies that attempted to micromanage market entry or control over a specific network or technology will usually have unintended consequences.

A good example of this can be found in the early history of the telecommunications industry, which was characterized by intense facilities-based competition until policymakers intervened. Once AT&T's original patents started expiring in 1893, its market dominance quickly waned. Independent competitors began springing up in areas not served by the Bell System and then quickly began invading AT&T's turf, especially in areas where Bell service was poor. According to telecom industry historian Gerald W. Brock, by the end of 1894 more than 80 new independent competitors had already grabbed 5 percent of total market share, and the number of independent firms continued to rise so dramatically that just after the turn of the century more than 3,000 competitors existed.[20] Illinois, Indiana, Iowa, Missouri, and Ohio each had more than 200 telephone companies competing within their borders.[21] By 1907, non-Bell firms continued to develop and were operating 51 percent of the telephone businesses in local markets. Prices were driven down as many urban subscribers were able to choose among competing providers. AT&T's profits and prices during this period began to shrink as a result of increased competition. Whereas AT&T had earned an average return on investment of 46 percent in the late 1800s, by 1906 their return had dropped to 8 percent.[22] As Brock notes, this competitive period brought gains unimaginable just a few years earlier:

> After seventeen years of monopoly, the United States had a limited telephone system of 270,000 phones concentrated in the centers of the cities, with service generally unavailable in the outlying areas. After thirteen years of competition, the United States had an extensive system of six million telephones, almost evenly divided between Bell and the independents, with service available practically anywhere in the country.[23]

Industry historians Leonard S. Hyman, Richard C. Toole, and Rosemary M. Avellis summarize the overall effect of this period by saying, "It seems competition helped to expand the market, bring down costs, and lower prices to consumers."[24] It is difficult to reconcile these findings with the oft-repeated natural monopoly claims made about this industry. Despite the significant sunk costs associated with market entry, rivals flooded the market and technological innovation flourished.

What then caused the eventual monopolization of the industry? A variety of direct and indirect government interventions.[25] Just before World War I, policymakers began taking steps to compel interconnection of competing systems that actually discouraged head-to-head, cutthroat competition. Brock found that "interconnection . . . eliminated the independents' incentive to establish a competitive long-distance system."[26] Huber et al. conclude, "The government solution, in short, was not the steamy, unsettling cohabitation that marks competition but rather a sort of competitive apartheid, characterized by segregation and quarantine."[27]

Worse yet, during World War I, the federal government nationalized the entire telecommunications system and began geographically averaging prices to artificially suppress rural rates. This created a serious disincentive for local telephone competition since few firms will seek to enter a market and offer service if they realize it is difficult, if not impossible, to undercut the subsidized service of the incumbent carrier. By the time the government privatized the industry again after the war, the combination of misguided interconnection policies and rate regulation had given AT&T the upper hand in its battle against independents. Eventually, the government allowed, and even encouraged, AT&T to buy up all of its competitors since policymakers came to endorse AT&T's corporate marketing slogan of "One Policy, One System, Universal Service" as official government policy.

The history of the telephone industry offers important insights that modern proponents of forced interconnection need to realize. Regulation can have unintended consequences and technological stasis should not be assumed. In this regard, natural monopoly and essential facility thinking has been most thoroughly critiqued by economists from the "Austrian School" of economics, such as Ludwig von Mises, Friedrich A. Hayek,[28] and Israel M. Kirzner.[29] These scholars have argued cogently that not only are answers to the questions about natural monopoly wrong, the questions themselves are improperly formulated. Competition, these scholars insist, is a dynamic process of constant entrepreneurial adjustment to market signals. The market is never at rest. At the very least, a truly competitive marketplace will be free of any artificial, government-created restraints or barriers to entry that interrupt the dynamic adjustment process. Hence, when one examines the development of the various markets thought to be natural monopolies or essential facilities, the "failure" at issue may not be that of the market, but of legislators and regulators who failed to allow entrepreneurial solutions to emerge.

Lastly, with respect to preemptive government regulation of supposed natural monopolies, an apparent contradiction emerges. There arises the troubling question of why economists would ever propose to restrict or control entry into new markets at all. As Thomas Hazlett has asked, "Why should we need to prevent entry when the market's own verdict is that only one firm shall survive? How is it that political agents are quicker and surer in their estimations of monopoly market structure than capital markets?"[30] This is illustrative of the regulatory hubris that riddled the centrally planned economies of the past century.

### Disregard of the Importance of Property Rights

A final problem with the concepts of natural monopoly and essential facilities is that they ignore any reference to property rights, freedom of creation, freedom of investment, and freedom of exclusion. This may be because the supporters of these concepts often oppose property rights and other capitalist freedoms in general. Or, it may be that they are simply reluctant to note how their philosophy ignores those rights in favor of more ambiguous societal goals that entail governmental coercion. An economic philosophy rooted in property rights, entrepreneurial freedom, and individual liberty rejects the forcible imposition of governmental orders on society or the economy at large. Instead, a capitalist ethos stresses the importance of spontaneous market evolution as well as voluntary interaction and agreements among private parties.

## Would Regulation Be the Best Approach Anyway?

Just for the sake of argument, what if we assume the critics are right and that natural monopolies really do exist? What does that entail for public policy? Some scholars—most notably those of the "Chicago School" of economic thinking—have argued that even if policymakers come to believe that network industries are natural monopolies, regulation should not automatically be assumed to be the superior alternative. Nobel Prize–winning economist Milton Friedman, for example, has gone so far as to argue that a private, unregulated monopoly should be tolerated before society opts for a regulated monopoly or state control of a specific industry or technology. Friedman advocates this policy prescription:

> Dynamic changes are highly likely to undermine it and there is at least some chance that these will be allowed to have their effect. And even in the short run, there is generally a wider range of substitutes than there seems to be at first blush, so private enterprises are fairly narrowly limited in the extent to which it is profitable to keep prices above cost.[31]

Similarly, in a now famous 1969 *Stanford Law Review* article, Judge Richard Posner, a senior lecturer at the University of Chicago Law School, provocatively argued, "It is not clear that an unregulated monopolist will normally charge a price that greatly exceeds what a nonmonopolist would charge for the same service; nor is it clear that society should be deeply concerned if a natural monopolist does charge an excessive price."[32] Because even if returns did run higher than normal for a given firm considered to possess a monopoly, Posner points out that this may act as a pro-competitive stimulus for innovation and market entry. "In the long run, a persistently very large spread between price and cost may spur entrepreneurs to devise ingenious methods of challenging or supplanting the monopolist," notes Posner.[33] Therefore, short-run intervention is likely to be counterproductive and to delay or prohibit the optimal long-run situation policymakers desire.

In other words, even though some firms may possess significant market power within a given industry sector during a given period of time, such moments will typically be fleeting so long as governments do not prop up market power artificially through entry and exit controls, price regulation, or restrictive licensing procedures. Sensing a profit-making opportunity, entrepreneurs will usually take notice and act when things seem to be at their worst within a given market, especially as new technologies emerge that make it easier to undercut the hegemony of firms that might have significant market power. As Viscusi et al. note, "In our technologically progressive world, there should be no presumption that an industry that is a natural monopoly today will be a natural monopoly tomorrow."[34]

Other scholars, such as Nobel Prize winners George J. Stigler and James Buchanan, have pointed out that regulation is typically a poor substitute for markets because of the problem of "regulatory capture" and "regulatory failure." Stigler noted in a seminal 1971 article in the *Bell Journal of Economics and Management Science* that "regulation is acquired by the industry and is designed and operated primarily for its benefit."[35] While Stigler's "capture" theory of regulation challenged conventional thinking at the time, it has been refined by many thinkers[36] and become more commonly accepted among modern economists.[37] Milton Friedman has similarly concluded that "regulatory agencies often tend themselves to fall under the control of the producers and so prices may not be any lower with regulation than without regulation."[38] And noted regulatory economist Alfred E. Kahn has likewise argued:

> When a [regulatory] commission is responsible for the performance of an industry, it is under never completely escapable pressure to protect the health of the companies it regulates, to assure a desirable performance by relying on those monopolistic chosen instruments and its own controls rather than on the unplanned and unplannable forces of competition.[39]

Judge Posner concurs, noting:

> Because regulatory commissions are of necessity intimately involved in the affairs of a particular industry, the regulators and their staffs are exposed to strong interest group pressures. Their susceptibility to pressures that may distort economically sound judgments is enhanced by the tradition of regarding regulatory commissions as "arms of the legislature," where interest-group pressures naturally play a vitally important role.[40]

Capture theory is just one of the many problems identified by economists that may contribute to regulatory failure more broadly. Richard H. K. Vietor has identified three primary sources of regulatory failure throughout economic history: (1) retention of regulations after technological change has made them irrelevant; (2) faulty design of the regulations that often work at cross-purposes; and

(3) procedural gridlock, misguided judicial precedents, and bureaucratic infighting, which delay or prohibit constructive change at regulatory agencies.[41]

In light of the concerns identified by these scholars, it is worth asking whether regulatory failure is, in the aggregate, worse than any perceived "market failure" that policymakers fear. Some modern proponents of industrial regulation—and forced-access mandates in particular—will behave as if regulation has moved into a new era that is free of such special-interest influence and regulatory capture concerns. As is discussed below, many regulators now purport to believe in the importance of competition and open markets but also claim that they must continue to regulate to bring about a more competitive state of affairs and redress the evils of the past. In addition, regulatory activity now appears to be more in line with the interests of new rivals than with those of the incumbents that once benefited from government intervention. In other words—or so the theory goes—we live in an era of "new and improved" publicly minded regulation that is free of the threat of capture by incumbent interests and less likely to produce anti-consumer results given the professed newfound faith in competition and markets supposedly held by many lawmakers and regulators.

These theories and arguments are really nothing new, however. Every generation has its proponents of benevolent bureaucracy and scientific management of the economy, but changing rhetoric or rationales for intervention cannot disguise the fact that today's "new and improved" public interest theory of regulation remains fundamentally flawed and susceptible to the same dangers it was in the past. As Lawrence White concludes, "The concept of the perfectly intervening government that only improves on market imperfections is . . . a textbook fiction; real-world governments too have their imperfections."[42] Indeed, this will always be the case regardless of the shifting rationales for regulatory interventions.

## Open Access as a Reparations Policy

Some scholars argue that open-access policies are a useful way to right the wrongs of the (regulatory) past—that is, to correct for the fact that some companies were given an unfair advantage through years of protected franchise monopolies and guaranteed rate-of-return regulation. Indeed, compared to cynical exploitation of open-access policy to hobble a competitor, there is some surface plausibility to this more traditional rationale for forced access. Governments at the federal, state, and local levels did indeed shield certain industries (electricity, telephony, cable television) from the pressures of competitive entry for many decades.

While this is a more plausible argument for forced access, once again the ends do not justify the means. Imposing such an economically inefficient regulatory regime on the marketplace to punish a handful of companies is hardly a sensible policy given the devastation it can wreak on the broader industry sector, consumers, or the economy as a whole.

As the case studies below on electricity and telecommunications make clear, attempting to punish incumbent firms ultimately hurts other rivals and consumers more than incumbent companies. That is because forced-access regulation breeds dependency on existing systems, resulting in numerous competitors haggling with network owners and regulators over the best terms of access to increasingly technologically obsolete networks of the past. While this helps policymakers create the short-term illusion of competition by allowing multiple companies to enter the market and offer service, the system will ultimately collapse under its own weight because infrastructure sharing and regulatory arbitrage do not represent very good business models or genuine competition.

Moreover, profit margins get squeezed very quickly with so many companies vying for space on existing systems, since regulators can only push access rates so low before investment and innovation seriously suffer. And if access prices are pushed perversely low, at some point the "inflationary bubble" of cheap network access will have to burst because older systems can only carry so much capacity. So, ironically, calls for forced access as incumbent punishment can backfire and end up hurting proponents more in the long run if they become too dependent on the regime.

In addition, supporters of open access as a reparations policy often fail to define how long the "punishment" should last. Are forced infrastructure-sharing requirements to last in perpetuity? When the Telecom Act was being developed in the mid-1990s, forced access was generally viewed as a transitional, second-best regulatory regime that would only last until such time as greater *facilities-based* competition developed within the local telephone marketplace. In fact, early drafts of the Telecom Act contained "date-certain" deregulatory provisions that completely deregulated the marketplace after two to three years. Ultimately, this more purely deregulatory approach was rejected simply because long-distance companies refused to sign off on the Act unless rules were included that either extended that date-certain transition for many additional years, or imposed some other method of hindering or punishing incumbents. That ultimately led to the inclusion of a "checklist" of open-access requirements that the incumbent local telephone companies would have to satisfy before any additional deregulatory freedoms would be granted.

While the potential scope and intent of some of the provisions were unclear, what was abundantly clear at the time was that the open-access regime was never intended to be a permanent part of the telecom landscape—it was supposed to be a halfway house on the road to pure market deregulation. Today, however, it has become an enshrined article of regulatory faith, a quasi-religious doctrine that proclaims that a numerical nose count of new entrants is more important than network investment and genuine facilities-based competition. But, again, basing the future of a given sector on such an ethos will eventually result in its ruin, since regulatory arbitrage can't work forever. Regulators may think this is a sensible way to restrain incumbents to rectify past unfair advantages, but in reality it only ends up hurting consumers who are denied serious facilities-based competition and better technological options.

Finally, as we move further away from the regulated utility model of the past and allow unrestricted entry into formerly regulated markets, corporate shareholders, not ratepayers, will be increasingly responsible for investment risks. Local telephone companies, cable companies, and electricity companies are all shareholder-owned entities. The risks inherent in the massive ongoing investments being made by these companies now fall squarely on the shoulders of the firms and their investors.

Although some of the underlying infrastructure of the regulated era of the past remains in place, it is increasingly becoming obsolete and is gradually being replaced. Billions of dollars of new investment is made every year by many of today's network industries *without* the assumption that the government and captive ratepayers will be there to bail them out in the future. A forced-access mentality, however, argues for a return to the methods of the past as costs are spread more widely throughout the industry, and networks are shared as a natural monopoly or an essential facility. This represents a step backward and entails constant regulatory oversight and intervention. Moreover, it raises the question—What good is a reparations policy that preserves the evils of the past?

# 3. Why Network Proliferation Spells the End of the Essential Facilities Doctrine

In spite of the natural monopoly mindset that has dominated regulatory economics, duplication, overlap, and redundancy seem to be the norm in networks where government regulation does not dominate. While natural monopoly theory posits that one firm quickly becomes dominant and capable of repelling all upstarts, ours is an era in which many network industries are building overlapping, redundant facilities or coming to a realization that doing so might make business sense. Where free to do so, networks seem to proliferate, heedless of the essential facilities doctrine. The proper policy goal is to allow the flowering of a marketplace capable of fostering reinforcement, enhancement, and expansion of new infrastructure—rather than promote open access to a given network. Aggressively pursued, the latter policy almost by definition freezes infrastructure where it stands. The forced-access model is a recipe for stagnation, not development.

Where a given network isn't designed for a particular application, upstarts face incentives to devise a new one. But open-access policies can interfere with those needs for flexibility and adaptation, encouraging market participants to simply make do with what exists. If adaptability and new infrastructure are critical, forced access can do considerable damage. For example, electricity grids were originally designed to allow small transactions between vertically integrated utilities, rather than the large flows of power between widely dispersed merchant generators and consumers that characterize the mandatory access regimes that proponents of restructuring favor. Likewise, cable and DSL networks were not designed for open access—nor even specifically for Internet access itself—and upgrading of both kinds of networks has been a priority. But if uninvited competitors are allowed aboard by regulators, network proprietors will be reluctant to transform themselves through improvements into the more suitable, tailored networks of tomorrow. Normal and healthy obsolescence of suboptimal technology will be impeded. Competition among network rivals can best foster cutting-edge advances. *Wired*, for example, referred to the reluctance of AT&T, Sprint, and WorldCom to aggressively seek to unify voice and data on a single network while newcomer Qwest explicitly sought that goal.[1] Troubled as it is now, Qwest's mission had been the financing of high-speed fiber networks thousands of miles long that feature buried, redundant, empty plastic conduits that would allow rapid installation of next-generation fiber, all to realize the goal of replacing circuit-switched networks with packet-switched ones on a national scale.[2]

New infrastructure is a welcome alternative to the business model of piggybacking on competitors' infrastructure. Qwest's mission, that of creating a 16,000-mile fiber network with buried empty conduits that can handle multiple lines, was a hard approach to square with the natural monopoly, one-line-is-enough model. Level 3 at one point was burying 10 conduits, leaving nine empty and available for later use.[3] (That hasn't stopped Level 3 from advocating open access to other companies' lines, however; businessmen do not necessarily stand accused of consistency and adherence to principle.[4])

Open-access regulatory policy cannot cope with the reality that a constant feature of any market is impermanence—that the entire current generation of technologies will occasionally need to be replaced with something new. Building networks can take time, but it is time well spent compared to the time, resources, and energy that can be wasted on forced access to an aging technology. For example, the telecommunications industry is gradually shifting to all-optical, packet-switched networks to replace the traditional circuit switching that ties up lines. And a number of businesses are proposing to bring fiber-optic cable to the home, or at least to the curb. Mandatory access delays this network evolution by regarding it as impractical or too expensive. It is not, but it may take time and patience. Along with refraining from access mandates, ending government-granted franchises and other distortionary regulation would increase opportunities for network industry growth and competition.

There is no clear winner in the race to create and own the networks of tomorrow—because if forced access is properly restrained, the networks of tomorrow don't necessarily exist yet. We know that new networks of various sorts need to be built; the policy issue is what model of competition and property rights is the proper way to get that ongoing job accomplished. In an evolutionary sense, it's a job that is never complete. Furthermore, forced access doesn't harm just the sector in which it is imposed; since cross-fertilization and shared investment *across* network industries could be important, imposing access in any one realm can have ripple effects across network industries by undermining opportunities for separate, unrelated network industries to work together and evolve in ways we may not envision today.

### Sharing Happens

When projects are too big and expensive for one company to undertake, the participation of more players may make sense. In other words, while it may be too expensive for a given company or industry, acting alone, to extend a network to the business or industrial park, the curb, or the customer's door, they may find it feasible if they band together with other companies or industries. For example, a nonutility power producer might team up with a phone company and real estate developers to share corridors and install power lines and telecommunications services to business customers, something now forbidden by many state laws that disallow power delivery by anyone other than the incumbent utility. Another synergy that already occurs is when an electric utility sells access to its rights-of-way to a telecommunications upstart to make new ventures possible. Here, the right-of-way is shared but not the wires.

Consortia have been responsible for planning ambitious ventures like the GlobalStar satellite network[5] and the proposed Teledesic satellite network.[6] Consortia are also responsible for the hundreds of thousands of miles of fiber-optic cable submerged in the oceans—enough to circle the equator several times.[7] In a less gigantic but still significant development, in some cases moving into telecommunications can be a natural extension for electric utilities thanks to their existing infrastructure of poles and wires and, often, fiber-optic networks.[8] Many have developed such networks as a byproduct of their own internal communications.

Efforts to join forces without regulatory pressure notably manifest themselves even in new industries without the history of regulatory central planning. Wireless cellular phone companies, for example, have often struck largely voluntary "roaming" deals to hand off phone calls to each other. Similarly, groups of wireless companies have joined forces to standardize the interface for mobile phones in order to create an attractive platform for the development of online wireless applications, a move that, if successful, would benefit them all.[9] (Developers currently must customize for individual manufacturers' handsets.) In another recent development, U.S. wireless carriers VoiceStream Wireless and Cingular Wireless agreed in the fall of 2001 to share their networks and the costs of upgrades—the first deal of its kind involving U.S. carriers.[10] Such developments make it clear that partial integrations are, or should be allowed to be, important features of networked economies. Sometimes full mergers or total infrastructure sharing won't be appropriate, while voluntary partial sharing agreements are.

Open-access regulation and disparate regulatory regimes within each sector can obscure the mechanisms by which network industries could be potential partners in building the infrastructures of the future and the avenues by which sensible and mutually advantageous open-access strategies can evolve on business's own terms. These potential competitive avenues should not be sealed off by further entrenchment of regulation. If producers simply gain mandatory interconnection to pre-existing networks, competitive pressures to undertake wiring or conduit installation or other infrastructure are undermined. Rethinking property rights to better appreciate such varieties of "long and thin" property may become increasingly important as arrangements become more complex. The onerous risks and complexities involved in network expansion will be made as attractive as possible by having lots of pots of gold at the ends of a number of rainbows.

Those pots of gold lead to the expected innovations. For example, telecommunications firms have long rented space in the tunnels of Washington, D.C.'s Metro subway system.[11] But sometimes, those pots of gold lead to some extreme examples of creativity. For example, underneath the nation's capital, Washington's 1,800 miles of sewers

> Are passages to Washington's past—and its future. Walking
> in knee-high rubber boots with a flashlight along a slick path,

> [inspector Floyd Patterson Jr.] points out a 65-year-old cast-iron sewer pipe. Above the city's sewers is a spaghetti of pipes, conduit, cables, concrete boxes and steam pipes, some dating to the 1800s. There are obsolete streetcar tracks from the first half of this century, replaced later by subway tunnels. Abandoned Western Union telegraph cables are close to new fiber-optic networks that will supply telephone, high speed Internet and other data services well into the next century.[12]

Taking creativity to new heights (or depths, as it were) is CityNet Telecommunications, a company whose business is installing fiber-optic cables in sewer systems using cylindrical video-equipped robots to string fiber through sewer mains, leaving road surfaces undisturbed.[13] (The destruction of above-ground property and esthetics is one of the long-held rationales for regulation.) The company has agreements in several cities.

Similarly, innovations such as computer-controlled horizontal directional drilling ought to make it easier for future deployment of network infrastructure around bottlenecks, flexibly snaking under streets and buildings, undercutting the case for open access as the technology becomes cheaper and more efficient. Horizontal boring is faster and causes less disruption to streets (although, since it's harder to tell where one is going and city underground detail maps may be less than optimal, other pipes can be damaged[14]). Some procedures leave a four-inch opening in place. If monopoly rights are eliminated, sideways directional drilling might be employed to bury low-voltage electric distribution lines in towns, which could bring costs down and raise partnership possibilities. This technique can be an attractive alternative to digging up a crowded city or residential street. Network firms could run their lines down the conduit in exchange for shouldering some of the costs.

### Networks Can Grow from *Both* Ends

An often-neglected feature of network industries is the fact that they have two end points. While the Internet-connected refrigerator and toaster have been overhyped, some remain bullish on consumer demand for home networking and high bandwidth, noting that broadband providers (like DSL and cable) as well as makers of consumer electronics, computers, games, network software, and security systems all are interested in connectivity for household

41

devices.[15] Although companies like Qwest and Level 3 and their descendants push outward with their fiber supply, not quite getting it to the curb, customer demand for such services can lead to a desire by customers to push outward toward the waiting fiber in novel ways. That can mean a profit opportunity for observant entrepreneurs.

For example, some firms are getting into the business of closing the gap, the "last mile," to the consumer by partnering with real estate developers. A company called ClearWorks Technologies is in the business of building high-tech wiring infrastructure for new homes in Houston and Las Vegas so that "owners can experience a commercial-quality technology infrastructure similar to what they have at work."[16] "Future-proofing" new homes with fiber is considerably cheaper than retrofitting—less than 1 percent of construction cost.[17] Basic and advanced wiring options encompass fast Internet, digital telephone with voice mail and caller ID, digital cable, closed circuit security, and online rental of videos and games. Of course, such ventures are going to face problems. They represent a new and untried business model. But the efforts are quite interesting. Another effort is that of builder John Laing Homes, who is constructing homes with high-speed data, and audio and video capability preinstalled during construction in nearly every room to provide enough bandwidth for any application. The cost of the wiring is included in the price of the home. Cable runs through the rooftop and attic for direct satellite, and PVC conduits are left in the walls for future wiring. The company's motto: "Retrofits are Hell."[18] Such developers are potential partners for network entrepreneurs.

As wires are extended to households, households could reach out on their own to meet those incoming wires. In a write-up about plastic—as opposed to glass—optical fiber, *Wired* notes, "Despite all the talk about fiber to the home, it looks like you're gonna have to lay it yourself." [19] Plastic would be cheaper and easier for home-owners to install.[20]

Demand-side growth is emerging from beyond the individual home. Increasingly, homeowners are likely to expect high-speed Internet access as they expect other fixtures like fireplaces and garages. That has led developers to respond by getting into the telecommunications business "either by building and owning neighborhood networks, or joining with telecommunications companies."[21] Builders are seeking an "ownership interest in the infrastructure" they are installing.[22] Toll Brothers, a high-end Pennsylvania dealer, builds and owns broadband networks within its developments, while other developers and telecommunications companies enter revenue-sharing agreements.[23] Since developers control the land, particularly in outer suburbs, they represent a growing threat to established cable and telecommunications firms, even as they represent an interesting new angle in solving the last-mile problem.

More substantial and robust competition will emerge if more precious years aren't wasted trying to *mandate* it. Because of the need to allow the most fertile ground possible for innovation, the role of policymakers, to the extent they have any role at all, is the opposite of their quest for mandatory access. They should disabuse market rivals of the promise of a free ride on others' networks. Instead their duty is to ensure that every producer in a free market understands that they're on their own, that no other partner—or rival—is obligated to help them succeed. While industries expand their networks, or perhaps form consortia to share rights-of-way and develop infrastructure, their cousins in other network industries may have a complementary interest in building out. At the same time, private groups such as homeowners' associations and other cooperatives may play an increasingly pivotal role as well in reaching "upward" to meet them.

CEOs should protest mandatory open access and convert themselves into "network entrepreneurs" open to the pursuit of new technologies and unexpected partnerships. Given the competitive pressures created by such an environment, incumbents faced with the threat of entry by a rival will often be induced to offer open access voluntarily. In other words, it would be foolish for firms to be so intransigent that they induce rivals to build competing networks within the same service territory. In many cases it would likely be better to strike a legitimate, *voluntary* open-access deal that everyone can live with than to be bypassed and left behind. Thus, under ordinary competition, the aims of advocates of forced open access will yet be realized, but in a market-driven manner. A by-product of such network industry competition is superior network reliability thanks to the proprietary interests of its creators and owners. Also compelling is the fact that rejecting the open-access model means policymakers will not need to revisit network industries to iron out distortions caused by the attempt to force competition, as has occurred in telecommunications. That industry, as will be seen in the next section, is clearly paying the price for embracing the "ideal" of open access.

America would be better served by fully deregulating network industries and taking our chances with potential, occasional exercises of transitory monopoly power than by erecting a *guaranteed* monopoly in the form of federal and/or state regulation of entire networks. Any lingering monopoly abuses that may occur under full deregulation are likely rooted not in the market process but in the residue of the prior government-granted monopoly that should never have existed in the first place.

PART II:

CASE STUDIES: HOW FORCED ACCESS HARMS
SPECIFIC INDUSTRIES

# 4. Case Study 1: Open Access to the Electricity Grid

*There is no upside, in the long run, [to] being dependent on your primary competitor for your key assets, or in relying on the Government to protect or subsidize your service.*

Federal Communications Commission Chairman
Michael Powell,[1] December 1998

Several experiments in forced-access regulation are currently under way. Most notably, such mandates currently govern or have been seriously proposed for industries such as electricity, telecommunications, broadband markets, cable and satellite networks, and computer operating software and instant messaging (IM) services. In all these cases, mandatory access threatens to undercut the evolution and reliability of services and to undermine business models that would entail network industries banding together to offer services. Since consumer protection is often the rationale for access mandates, their inappropriateness and inevitable failure are even more regrettable.

The effort to reform the nation's $228 billion electricity industry has long been a victim of open-access disease, given such measures as the Energy Policy Act of 1992, which stipulated mandatory access to the grid for wholesale power exchanges, and 1978's Public Utility Regulatory Policy Act, designed to combat the energy crisis by mandating purchases by utilities from favored power producers, such as those generators using renewable energy.[2] The drive for access has created complications and ongoing debates over central management that have stalled deregulation of this industry for many years, and threatens to distort the industry so thoroughly as to make the emergence of free, efficient, reliable markets impossible. In their calls for mandatory open access in electricity, would-be reformers from both political parties make the typical high-sounding populist promise: that every commercial, residential, or industrial customer should have their choice of any electricity provider. The local utility, however, would be forced to distribute the new provider's electricity over its wires. Therein lies the problem, and therein lies the departure from actual deregulation.

In March 2002, the Supreme Court upheld the 1996 Federal Energy Regulatory Commission (FERC) order implementing the 1992 Energy Policy Act by requiring utilities to open their wholesale wire networks to competitors on the same terms they provide to themselves, further reinforcing the principle of federal jurisdiction over the networks.[3] (Ironically, the embattled Enron Corporation had argued that the order didn't go far enough in mandating access to all retail transmissions—that it should cover transactions in which the cost of electricity was bundled, in a single price, with the cost of transmission. In this and in other ways, Enron was hardly the advocate of deregulation that its reputation once implied.[4] Enron's argument for expanding open access to all retail transmissions was rejected.[5])

As noted, open-access policies require price controls and central management, policies that have visibly plagued restructuring in California.[6] Political management means that core issues of governance and control over property—which require market resolution—remain as hotly debated as ever. Among those issues are state versus federal jurisdiction; the role of so-called "independent system operators" in managing the power grid; the role of public power in a restructured market; and "stranded cost" recovery sought by utilities seeking to recover their investment in regulator-approved power projects that may be made obsolete by competitive bypass.[7]

In the aftermath of the California fiasco, federal electricity reform—which would allow consumers to choose their electricity provider but force the local incumbent to deliver—is off the table in Congress (despite the efforts of groups like the Electricity Consumers Resource Council, which has been pushing for "retail wheeling" of electricity since the 1980s). Ironically, even the most ambitious federal open-access bills would have allowed several years after enactment before open access would fully take effect. That's a long time to wait when the end result would simply be a socialized power grid.

The industry remains paralyzed in uncertainty, not knowing where policy is headed in the coming years. Actual deregulation, not subordinate to expectations of forced access, would lead to greater certainty, investment, and results. A policy environment that promotes voluntary entrepreneurial interconnections, not central management by the system operators, is called for. Yet today FERC is at work on establishing monopolistic "regional transmission organizations."[8]

In the electricity marketplace, competition requires abolishing exclusive local service territories and letting competitors go at it. Namely, the right of competitors to erect or bury their own competing wires and serve captive customers, if they can figure out a way to do it, should undergird policy perspectives. Producers should have the right to sell the electricity they generate to whomever they choose. But how they get the power to the customer is a private problem, not something for regulators to solve. Instead, artificial barriers that prohibit *voluntary* competition—the state-granted exclusive local service territories that protect incumbents—should be removed. So long as delivery monopolies remain intact, a homeowners' association or business park deploying microturbines, for example, could find itself in violation of franchise laws. Similarly, possibilities for cross-industry consortia like those noted in the last chapter would be forestalled. Such artificial barriers are incompatible with competition.

Removing statutory monopoly rights would grant to entrepreneurs, adventurous electric utitlities, and independent power producers the clout to cut voluntary access deals and develop infrastructure by forming, buying, or sharing rights-of-way with network industry cousins such as telecommunications and railroad firms. An independent power producer might join a Bell company and real estate developers to share the costs of providing electricity and communications services to residential and business customers.

Advocates of open access ignore the principle that innovation in transmission and distribution is as crucial as any other kind of innovation. The right approach to fostering competition can set in motion an industry restructuring that is as fully efficient and entrepreneurial as possible, one in which entrepreneurs rather than captive ratepayers bear the risks. Years would be saved, since the need for future legislation to correct distortions caused by forced access would be minimized. When all is said and done, the proper market structure lies somewhere on a continuum between central generation

and long-distance transmission on the one hand and on-site generation with zero transmission on the other. Only market interaction
can locate that point. Indeed, the market will likely reveal that this
point changes constantly.

A host of innovations show noteworthy promise for posing competitive threats to incumbent utilities without resorting to access
mandates. However, if rival generators can simply dump the electricity they generate into the grid at a regulated fee, such innovation
could be ended before it begins. Although it may be an anathema
to open access advocates, the ability to exclude rivals can have an
important impact on the development and profitability of proprietary technologies like those noted below. Uncertainty regarding
politicized restructuring unfortunately prolongs their rollout.

### Smaller-Scale and Aggressive Generation

Smaller, natural gas–powered generators with the promise of
threatening central station utilities' comfortable lock on generation
have helped inspire today's clamor for competition. In response,
utilities are employing "distributed generation"—often modular,
self-contained units much smaller than existing central generating
plants that can be sited closer to the end user. These typically range
in size from 60,000 kW down to microturbines of about 5 kW.[9] (The
average giant central-station coal-fired plant is about 500,000 kW.[10])
Distributed options include diesel engines, combustion turbines,
microturbines, photovoltaic arrays, various forms of fuel cells, and
battery storage.

Traditional utilities are defensively exploiting these technologies
to meet peak demand without building new transmission or investment in more central plants, to serve remote customers, and to
improve customer relationships with new services and improved
quality and reliability.[11] In a sense, there already are two grids: the
power grid and the natural gas pipeline network. Generation closer
to the user means that sometimes it will be natural gas, not electricity,
that will be transported long-distance.

Microturbines could potentially bypass the grid altogether.
Weighing a few hundred pounds and often sporting only a single
moving part, microturbines of less than 1 MW can furnish on-site
power, such as servicing a 7-Eleven or a large home. Examples have
included Allied Signal's 75-kW TurboGenerator (McDonald's is one

famous customer), and microturbines produced by Allison Engine (owned by Rolls-Royce) and Capstone.

Trends toward smaller-scale generation are probably the most significant change confronting the power industry, and they help undercut the case for forced access. It's easy to envision hospitals, commercial firms, shopping malls, high-technology firms, and Internet service providers running sensitive electronic equipment requiring uninterrupted power embracing microturbines. Indeed, many already do. Single or stacked units in buildings and, in the long run, along new streets (perhaps ultimately displacing utility-owned distribution lines) may be in the offing, helping improve reliability.

In 1998, RKS Research & Consulting noted evidence of a "major shift from the model of central station plants and poles and wires to a new paradigm of small, decentralized power and networked control systems. The shift could rival the change in computing from the mainframe to the desktop and network server in social and economic significance."[12] They further noted that one-fourth of businesses are troubled by periodic fluctuations and outages, and one-fifth are willing to pay 10 percent premiums for solutions.[13] If the industry truly is at a turning point, and if customer dissatisfaction is a central fact, then firms other than existing distribution utility monopolies must be allowed into the marketplace to serve consumers. Ending exclusive distribution rights would prevent utilities from parlaying monopoly power into domination of distributed generation, as open access unfortunately may allow them to do. Utilities' government-protected advantage over competitors—and over captive customers—should end before mass-produced small-scale generation and microturbines proliferate in the marketplace.

An additional technological and economic incentive for the adoption of smaller-scale generation is heat recovery. Heat is a "waste" product of electricity generation. Recovery of that waste heat for purposes of heating offices, universities, hospitals, and other facilities increases efficiency by making fuller use of the fuel burned.

### Improved Technological Control of Power Flows

Along with the claims that the grid is a natural monopoly, one rationale for continued regulation has been that electric power simply flows where it wants. One former deputy Energy secretary, in discussing the "tug of war" over deregulation by state and federal authorities, noted that "Electricity markets do not behave according to political boundaries" and that "Electrons don't respect borders."[14]

While today's bulk power system indeed operates under constraints for which design and operation must allow, it's less true now that electrons won't respect borders—if we want those borders respected. The development of silicon-based switches for high power loads shows promise for improving technological control over power flows. Switching power electronically rather than mechanically can allow efficient producers to extend their reach.[15] Improved control of power flows on the grid might be thought of as paralleling the control of small currents on a computer chip, itself a tiny "grid."

So far, electronic switching technology is best used where lines are loaded and restrict options for power marketing. A study of the use of a flexible AC transmission system (FACTS) control system on the Georgia-Florida transmission bottleneck "found that for roughly a $25-million to $30-million investment in FACTS controllers, power transferred between these states could be increased from 3,400 to 4,100 megawatts. That's an increase of 21 percent, which would yield roughly $130 million per year in additional revenues."[16]

Note that improved grid control pulls the industry in the opposite direction from microturbines because (1) better grid power management enhances the capacity, reliability, and stability of central-station generation and (2) it raises the value of central-station generation and long-range transmission as it now stands, relative to the widespread adoption of distributed generation and microgeneration. However, again, regulation is not the best means for pinpointing the proper balance between the two managerial approaches; ending franchise protections and allowing natural market development can move the market toward the best allocation of generation and transmission infrastructure. With regard to high-power electronics, one might reasonably argue that the grid remains largely uncontrollable today partly *because* it is regulated and little competition exists. Granting that, forced access could further lessen market pressures to adopt grid-control innovations, since individual firms' profits would be less likely to urgently depend on controlling power flows because they can just piggyback on a rival's system. Allowing markets to adjust to accommodate an ever-changing industry structure can make transmission more efficient than it has ever been, rendering the existing grid increasingly antiquated. Installing such networks or extensions will be expensive undertakings to say the least, but they are best fostered in an environment in which the builders can prosper. Again, entrepreneurs rather than captive ratepayers bear the risk.

### Power Line Communications

While not a competitor to electricity service, new innovations in power line communications propose to deliver high-speed Internet service over power lines.[17] For the time being, the technology faces considerable engineering difficulties. For example, a historical grid layout that employs fewer transformers near individual households has made the technology more adaptable to some countries in Europe, Asia, and South America.[18] It is far more problematic to work around the numerous near-the-user transformers common in the United States. Key to solving the problem, though, is the promise of rewards—particularly to the extent that powerline communications technology is faster than cable or DSL Internet service. Utilities have long used the technology within their networks for internal purposes such as meter reading communications.[19] Open-access policies that would dampen the present value of expanded investments in this cutting-edge technology would be a mistake, helping to ensure that the technology, assuming it would prove viable, never arrives at all.

### User Ownership of Power Networks

In addition to fostering competition between the competing visions of the central-station and distributed generation, phasing out exclusive franchises stokes customers' own incentives to exercise control over critical network assets. That desire fits in with the theme mentioned earlier of networks having two end points. For example, large power users, such as a manufacturing plant or a consortium of businesses in a high-tech office park, could purchase portions of the grid themselves, thereby entirely eliminating any risk of price gouging.[20]

### Threats and "Rifle Shot" Access

Given the array of competitive forces and technologies at hand, it would seem that deal-making with rivals, and perhaps even threats from rivals, can go a long way toward opening markets. There is likely to be little shortage of competitive pressures if franchises are ended, since any intransigent utility—in a marketplace in which its rate of return is no longer guaranteed by a captive customer base and a protected franchise—that refuses to offer reasonable access to a rival will likely face retaliation when it tries to expand. At most, as a temporary measure, when bottlenecks cannot be overcome in a reasonable amount of time and there is a legitimate threat of customer abuse stemming from the historical monopoly status of the utility, temporary "rifle shot" requirements for forced access might be considered by the states. But that should be the exceptional case; open access cannot be justified as a *universal* model, a restructuring regime to be imposed on an entire industry. Any access requirement must sunset; private control of the bottleneck in question should be sought as soon as possible in order to provide the proper incentives to maintain or expand infrastructure for future needs.

# 5. Case Study 2: Open Access to Local Telephone Networks

With the passage of the Telecommunications Act of 1996,[1] Congress granted the FCC sweeping new powers to conduct the most extensive experiment with forced-access regulation to date. Although Sections 251 and 252 of the Telecom Act took up only a few pages of the 200-plus-page bill, these access-related provisions have spawned an avalanche of regulatory and judicial paperwork and forced the industry to familiarize itself with an entirely new lexicon of regulatory terminology (interconnection, unbundling, collocation, reciprocal compensation, line sharing, line splitting, line conditioning, etc.) and acronyms (e.g., UNE, UNE-P, TELRIC, OSS).

The complexity of this new regulatory regime for local telephony is sometimes staggering. The FCC's now-fabled August 1996 Local Competition Order, for example, weighed in at an amazing 737 pages and contained more than 3,200 footnotes.[2] The edict, which ranks as one of the longest and most convoluted rules in the history of regulatory policymaking in America, contained a long list of specific elements owned by incumbent local exchange carriers (ILECs) that were to be subject to unbundling requirements under FCC-determined price regulations, including local loops, local switching capability, tandem switching capability, packet-switching capability, interoffice transmission facilities, databases and signaling systems, operator services, and directory assistance services.[3] This long list of items subject to sharing mandates and open-access price controls proved so contentious that it produced a stream of litigation that continues today. In fact, the Supreme Court has been forced to hand down two major decisions dealing with these regulations, *AT&T v. Iowa Utilities Board*[4] (examining the scope of infrastructure sharing requirements) and *Verizon Communications v. FCC* (examining the pricing methodology behind those sharing mandates).[5] Because of litigation and continuing questions about the applicability of these mandates to other services,[6] the agency has been forced to issue many other regulations regarding how open access will work in America's local telephone marketplace.

### The Return of Price Controls

More disturbing than the sheer volume of FCC rulemaking is the nature of much of this regulation. As part of their quixotic and seemingly never-ending efforts to determine the "fair" price of interconnection to, and resale of, the incumbents' networks, the FCC and state regulators have regressed to the heavy-handed regulatory schemes of the past. As Brookings Institution senior fellow Robert Crandall notes, the FCC's new interconnection regulatory regime "casts the Commission back into the business of cost-based regulation, but this time with a vengeance."[7] This has meant the reemergence of a de facto regime of price controls of communications services.

For example, the TELRIC (Total Element Long-Run Incremental Cost) pricing methodology that the Commission adopted in its Local Competition Order to price access to local facilities was based entirely on the hypothetical cost of deploying a new network from scratch, without any regard for historical investments or actual costs. This opened a Pandora's box of regulatory hijinks as the FCC and state regulators engaged in what is essentially crystal ball gazing and blatant guesswork to determine cost recovery schemes for communications carriers. As Eli Noam, professor of economics and finance at the Columbia Business School, has aptly summarized, "'Cost,' of course, is a concept that has induced much human creativity."[8] The FCC's TELRIC methodology certainly must rank as one of the most creative of all regulatory models in this regard. As Noam concludes, under TELRIC "cost is often calculated on the basis of impenetrable engineering models that Lenin would have liked if he only had had computers."[9]

More profoundly, Alfred Kahn, former chairman of the Civil Aeronautics Board, has referred to the logic behind TELRIC as "regulatory arrogance," and noted that:

> By their meddling, under enormous pressure to produce politically attractive results, regulators have violated the most basic tenets of efficient competition—that it should be conducted on the basis of the respective actual incremental costs of the contending parties; and it is that competition, rather than regulatory dictation, that should determine the results.[10]

And technology guru George Gilder[11] has argued, "Like any price-control scheme, TELRIC choked off supply, taking the profits out of the multibillion-dollar venture of deploying new broadband pipes."[12] Moreover, Gilder adds, open access and unbundling mandates discourage broadband investment by "privatizing the risks and socializing the rewards. No entrepreneurs will invest in risky, technically exacting new infrastructure when they must share it with rivals."[13]

Regulators, and the industry rivals that support this forced-access regulation, argue that such rules are necessary because the communications marketplace is static and unchanging. They argue that ILECs have facilities in place to deliver service today that are unlikely to be duplicated any time soon and, therefore, all the components of the system must be completely unbundled and shared. Likewise, any extensions of this network—such as DSL services to provide broadband Internet access—must also be shared because rivals will not likely be able to make those facilities available either.

### An Increasingly Contestable Market

Supporters of forced access are wrong on both counts. Credible facilities-based competition to the imbedded voice network has developed in recent years, primarily from wireless sources. In an important study in the August 1999 edition of the *Hastings Law Journal*, economists J. Gregory Sidak, fellow in law and economics at the American Enterprise Institute, Hal J. Singer, senior vice president of Criterion Economics, and David J. Teece, professor at the Haas School of Business at the University of California–Berkeley, argue that "Wireless local telephony already provides a substitute for wireline access."[14] The authors ask:

> If wireless is indeed an access substitute for wireline copper loops, and if wireless thus permits the competitive supply of bundled services that are satisfactory substitutes in consumers' minds for the typical bundle of services that consumers have until now demanded in conjunction with standard wireline access, then Congress, the FCC, the state public utilities commission, and the courts must ask: Is the great experiment of mandatory unbundling of telecommunications networks worth the candle?[15]

Indeed, while wireless telephony has until recently only been considered a complement to wireline voice services, recent FCC surveys of wireless and wireline competition reveal that "there is growing evidence that consumers are substituting wireless service for traditional wireline communications. . . . Several local carriers have attributed declining access line growth rates in part to substitution by wireless."[16] A January 2002 *USA Today*/CNN/Gallup poll confirmed this gradual shift, noting that 18 percent—almost one in five—of cell phone owners surveyed consider their cell phones to be their "primary phone" today.[17] In 5 to 10 years, "The vast majority of us are going to be using wireless phones as our main phones," noted telecom analyst Jeff Kagan in the *USA Today* story.[18]

Two recent studies predict a continued shift to wireless. IDC, a global technology industry analysis firm, projected that consumers will continue to opt for wireless services over wireline options and that this will result in the displacement of 20 million wireline access lines by 2005.[19] IDC attributes this shift to falling prices, improved geographic service quality, and the popularity of bundled pricing programs that provide evening and weekend local and long-distance calling at little or no additional cost. Likewise, Telecompetition, Inc., a telecommunications networks and services forecasting firm, recently predicted that wireless and cable telephone service providers will steal 30 million access lines away from wireline carriers over the next five years.[20]

That reality is already being reflected in the fact that wireline access lines and minutes of use are no longer growing. *Forbes* magazine recently reported that nine million local phone lines were cut off in America in 2001, a 4.7 percent decline in the total number of phone lines from the year before.[21] Consumers are substituting buckets of wireless minutes for traditional local and long-distance wireline service, and some are even "cutting the cord" as they find they no longer need wireline service in their homes.

It is important to note that the cellular industry has accomplished this amazing feat without extensive direction or assistance from regulators. Unlike their wireline competitors, cellular firms face no unbundling requirements or price controls and yet facilities-based competition flourishes. According to the Cellular Telecommunications and Internet Association (CTIA) Web site,[22] as of October 2002, almost 140 million Americans subscribed to wireless cellular services, and average monthly bills have fallen by almost 50 percent over the last 10 years. Moreover, almost all Americans have an average of three to four wireless service providers at their disposal and, in some regions, as many as seven or eight competitive alternatives.[23] In other words, despite the absence of forced-access mandates in the wireless sector, companies have invested billions and full-fledged competition has thrived.

Regarding the second argument made by supporters of forced access—that regulators must guarantee rivals access to emerging wireline faculties and technologies in addition to older network components—Robert Crandall and Massachusetts Institute of Technology economist Jerry A. Hausman have argued:

> Today's network is not static—it is steadily evolving into new, more advanced networks, such as those designed to deliver high-speed Internet services. If an incumbent local network operator leases part of its current network to its rivals, will it be able to adopt new technology without these rivals' (entrants') assent? Surely, one would not want these new competitors using the regulatory process simply to delay or frustrate their rivals' attempts to innovate.[24]

Yet, that is exactly what has already happened and may happen with advanced communications offerings. Rivals have sought to game the system to their advantage, and, so far, regulators have been all too eager to oblige. Essentially, regulators have created a complex system of regulatory arbitrage that allows competitive local exchange carriers (CLECs) to free-ride on the incumbent's network without regard to the true cost of doing so. And now they are seeking to expand the system to include advanced communications services and networks that the Telecommunications Act of 1996 did not mention or envision.

### A Free-Rider's Paradise

Because the FCC has ensured that access to existing facilities is priced well below cost, the logical consequence of this regulatory regime was an initial increase in the overall number of new "competitors" serving the market. Correspondingly, however, this also meant that new rivals opted for infrastructure sharing over infrastructure building. Not being patient enough to wait for true facilities-based innovation and investment to develop, regulators instead "opted for quick, ephemeral results—a superficial froth of resale competition—over the substance of real competition based on newly built facilities,"[25] argues John Thorne, senior vice president and deputy general counsel of Verizon. "The Commission was more interested in counting noses than in counting networks," he rightly concludes.[26]

Therefore, while the ostensible purpose of all of this regulatory activity has been to create and maintain credible competitors to the ILECs, the FCC has instead simply created a small cottage industry of corporate free-riders without serious business plans or chances for long-term survival.[27] There is nothing wrong with *voluntary* wholesale/resale arrangements between incumbents and new carriers, but current forced-access mandates have artificially encouraged rivals to flock to the reselling option and to largely ignore facilities-based alternatives. That local access has led to inevitable disputes about "anti-competitive practices" with respect to treatment of alternative DSL providers, who claim incumbent discrimination.[28]

Mandated free-riding has proven to be a disastrous industrial policy for companies and consumers alike. As Supreme Court Justice Stephen Breyer pointed out in his 1999 opinion in *AT&T Corp. v. Iowa Utilities Board*, "It is in the *un*shared, not in the shared, portions of the enterprise that meaningful competition would likely emerge. Rules that force firms to share *every* resource or element of a business would create, not competition, but pervasive regulation, for the regulators, not the marketplace, would set the relevant terms."[29]

Heedless of the warning in Justice Breyer's opinion, new companies have been led to believe that network sharing can offer them a profitable and sustainable business model. And consumers have been led to believe that a temporary increase in the number of service providers means they have real competitive choices at their disposal. Regrettably, these twin myths continue to wreak havoc on the telecommunications sector.

### Markets Aren't Fooled

Luckily, investors and markets seems to be keenly aware of the negative effects of network sharing even if regulators are not. Robert Crandall, in an important recent Criterion Economics survey of CLEC stock market returns, found that "CLECs are best able to produce revenue growth by building their own networks or significant parts of their own networks. CLECs that only resold the established carriers' services were generally unable to convert investments into revenues, and these companies were likely to fail."[30] He continues:

> Leasing facilities from the established carriers or reselling
> their services can work as *part* of an entrant's business
> strategy.... Doing so allows an early jump-start over those
> building from scratch, but ultimately revenues grow more
> rapidly if the entrants build their own networks.[31]

In other words, markets are sending policymakers a clear message: *business models that are heavily dependent on a forced-access regulatory regime are not sustainable.*[32] Facilities-based CLECs are more likely to be able to weather difficult market conditions. As Mark Kastan, an analyst with Credit Suisse First Boston, argues, "You need to own your own network to have a viable business plan" in today's marketplace.[33]

Two simple conclusions can be drawn from the forced-access experiment that has taken place in the communications marketplace since 1996. First, forced-access regulation has created not a class of credible facilities-based competitors but a group of regulatory opportunists that have taken advantage of a convoluted legal regime of mandates and price controls to hitch a free ride on other carriers' networks. The most credible facilities-based competitors that have arisen to challenge the hegemony of incumbent local telephone giants have been wireless cellular providers, which are unregulated and were almost completely ignored by the Telecom Act. Second, forced-access regulation has discouraged investment in network upgrades and deployment, especially by incumbent carriers, who fear that the application of unbundling and line-sharing mandates on new services will prevent them from recovering the exorbitantly high fixed costs of network service. As Thomas M. Jorde, professor of law at the University of California–Berkeley, and his co-authors J. Gregory Sidak and David Teece argue:

> Mandatory unbundling decreases an ILEC's incentive to
> invest in upgrading its existing facilities by reducing the ex
> ante payoffs of such investment. Requiring a firm to grant
> to its competitors unbundled access to its facilities at TELRIC-
> based rates greatly reduces, if it does not eliminate entirely,
> the probability of excess return; such mandatory unbundling
> thus eliminates the ILEC's incentive to invest in existing
> facilities. It makes no economic sense for the ILEC to invest
> in technologies that lower its marginal costs, so long as com-
> petitors can achieve identical savings by regulatory fiat.[34]

61

### The Toll of Infrastructure Socialism

The overall macroeconomic devastation caused by forced-access regulation has been powerfully critiqued by Scott C. Cleland, CEO and founder of Precursor Group, a leading Washington, D.C.–based investment research organization specializing in telecommunications and high-technology sector investment trends:

> Unfortunately, the Telecom Act and FCC implementation have turned out to be a bipartisan economic disaster contributing to the severity and length of the economic downturn in telecom-tech. At the most basic economic level, the Government set wholesale prices *below real cost* in the high-fixed cost, price-inelastic local access market segment, poisoning prospects for economically sound *facilities investment*. Unintentionally, Government telecom policy is contributing to the destruction of companies, jobs, and shareholder wealth by discouraging economic investment and rewarding uneconomic investment.[35]

Likewise, Manhattan Institute senior fellow Peter Huber has argued that, in a sense, the Telecom Act's effort to encourage new entry at the expense of incumbents worked well, but precisely because it did, the long-term prognosis for true competition in this sector looks dim. Huber notes:

> The incumbents lost heavily, as they leased out more of their networks at tomorrow's theoretical prices, rather than at yesterday's actual costs. Local markets were crowded with new entrants who hadn't built much, if anything, in the way of new facilities, but who were vying to deliver more local traffic, and high-speed data traffic, to long-distance networks.[36]

Traffic volume increased as regulators depressed costs, which led many other companies to build their business models on the inflated expectations of artificial demand. "It couldn't last, and it didn't," Huber argues. "By making entry artificially cheap for everyone else, regulators attracted hoards of naive, spendthrift competitors, which made competition unprofitable for all."[37] Consequently, a number of resellers, fiber-optic companies, ISPs, and long-distance firms were forced to declare bankruptcy or go under completely.

## A Sunset Plan for Forced Access in Telecom Markets

In light of how miserably the experiment with forced-access regulation in the local telephone marketplace has failed, it would seem that policymakers would be eager to take steps to reopen the Telecom Act and address its deficiencies. Regrettably, however, the regulatory status quo remains firmly entrenched as no serious proposals to alter the Telecommunications Act of 1996 are currently pending before Congress. Furthermore, federal and state efforts to force further Bell "breakups" into wholesale and resale components, while not the same as forcing access to wires, have the same access goal; they seek to create an artificial regulatory structure that imposes access by more extreme measures.[38]

An alternative approach—assuming policymakers eventually come to recognize the destructive nature of current forced-access mandates—would be for legislators to draw up a sunset plan for open-access regulation within the telecom marketplace. As was mentioned in Chapter 5, early drafts of the Telecommunications Act contained provisions that demanded the local marketplace be completely deregulated by a "date certain." Those provisions were ultimately stripped from the draft bill in favor of the open-access language contained in Sections 251 and 252 of the Act. No one at the time believed that this language was intended to create a massive new and perpetual regulatory regime to supplant the previous system. Instead, open access was intended to be a halfway house on the road to pure market deregulation. The intent was to allow new entrants to "get a foot in the door" in the market by using the infrastructure owned by incumbents until such time as they could construct their own facilities.

Regrettably, however, the belief that forced access was merely a transitional device was never clearly written into law. Consequently, there are no provisions in the Telecom Act that terminate the access regime for telecommunications at any specific time in the future. But for all the reasons outlined above, infrastructure socialism must eventually end in this marketplace. Toward that end, policymakers should look to the example of how interconnection was gradually phased out of the wireless sector.

When analog cellular systems were first authorized by the FCC in the 1980s, only two licenses were awarded per geographic market. One of the two licenses was awarded to the incumbent wireline provider in each market. Because they were considered to possess a substantial advantage over the second licensee, who did not own wireline systems in the area, the FCC mandated that the incumbent wireline carriers allow the competing wireless licensee to resell cellular service on the incumbent's network.

But in 1992 the FCC decided to implement a firm cutoff date for resale access mandates on the wireless systems owned by incumbent telephone companies. Huber et al. note, "The rule was designed to address the problem of nonwireline licensees relying exclusively on resale service instead of building their own systems."[39] The FCC recognized the detrimental impact that perpetual sharing mandates would have on the deployment of analog cellular infrastructure and decided to sunset such resale rules after a five-year build-out period. A similar resale requirement for digital cellular licenses that was imposed in 1996 expired in November 2002. Meanwhile, innovative interconnection, roaming, and billing arrangements continue to be voluntarily hammered out through private negotiations between wireless carriers. Somehow, the proverbial sky has not fallen despite the lack of regulatory oversight and intervention at every turn.

The wisdom of the FCC's decision for wireless markets should be applied to the wireline market. Some critics will say it's "too soon" to sunset infrastructure-sharing mandates, but policymakers have already given open-access rules more than five years to work in the local telecom marketplace and the results have not been encouraging. To give all players fair warning, legislators could give them all another year or two to prepare for the end of the infrastructure-sharing regime to which they have grown accustomed. Legislators could set a date—say, January 1, 2004 or 2005—on which the regime of resale and line-sharing rules will expire. And then they could let the forced-access experiment in local telecom markets come to an end once and for all.

# 6. Case Study 3: Open Access to Broadband Services

*If we had four or five broadband pipes into every home in America, we wouldn't be having this [open access] discussion. That's where we need to go as a country.*

Former Federal Communications Commission
Chairman William Kennard[1]

Broadband services—or high-speed Internet and data access—are so varied and at such an embryonic stage that it seems astonishing that policymakers presume themselves capable of devising workable policies on open access. Yet they are only too happy to intervene in emergent markets. Part of the logic behind such proposals is the Internet's status as an "open" medium that anyone can view and within which anyone can communicate. Therefore, proponents of open access argue, the networks over which the Internet runs should also be "open" to any and all traffic. As the pro–forced access OpenNet Coalition argues on its Web site, "For consumers, the threat in this model is that the broadband network will be a closed, proprietary network, and will differ dramatically from the open, non-discriminatory access they enjoy today."[2] In other words, private network owners should not have the right of excludability; whether they like it or not they must all submit to common carrier–style regulation. Other supporters of forced access are fond of using highway analogies to make their case, as Andrew Schwartzman, president and CEO of the Media Access Project, does when he says, "We're at a fork in the information superhighway. . . . One way leads to open access, boundless innovation and free expression. The other has us follow the same path that made cable TV the closed, unresponsive, and overpriced monopoly Americans have grown to hate."[3]

The tendency to regard the allocation and pricing of others' property as theirs to dictate is characteristic of interventionists. The flaw in that viewpoint—apart from the seizure it entails—is the unwillingness to realize that there is no fixed highway; networks are evolving continually. Under open-access regulation, that feature of markets is to be ignored and sacrificed for the sake of redistributing wealth and regulating prices *now*. The effect of such ideas will be to freeze incentives to roll out new capacity, which helps ensure that future "highways" won't emerge at all. Companies won't innovate unless there is a reward for doing so. Thus, flexibility in pricing is also important for network deployment, and high rates on the new services at the dawn of this industry may well be necessary to bring in new investment—and, in turn, lower prices. To the interventionist, high prices are intolerable, despite their being transitory and critical to network deployment.

Patience is especially important because today's broadband speeds aren't really all that "broad." For example, cable modem services and teleco-provided DSL services are not "zippy" enough for future multimedia needs compared with what optical fiber can deliver. Policymakers must bear in mind, however, that neither cable modem nor DSL was designed for the Internet. For example, cable broadband, designed in loops of roughly 1,000 homes, is plagued by congestion and speed degradation as users sign up, which leads to the need to install more loops.[4] It will take years of work to develop the broadband network infrastructure to fit tomorrow's overwhelming demands. Mandatory access does not solve what are genuine technical problems. Interestingly, the dial-up modems that still serve as the gateway to the Internet for most Americans are the only unshared gateway; with both cable and DSL, access is shared with others, and as usage grows, speeds are compromised.[5] The fact that today's technologies are not optimal implies that market conditions capable of fostering the development of infrastructure designed specifically for a fast-paced online world must be preserved. Fiber to the home or satellite service, for example, might serve consumers better—and the incentives to build those advanced services must not be overwhelmed by mandatory access policies.

The rate of deployment of cable and DSL broadband services already seems to be affected by the threat of open-access mandates, and intervention-minded politicians and regulators should take note. According to recent FCC surveys, cable companies are the leading broadband providers, with about 70 percent of the market.[6]

Economist Dennis Carlton notes that cable modem service has far outpaced the rate of deployment of DSL service by local phone companies despite cable's typical status as a monopoly. The reason seems to be that, so far, cable companies do not face general open-access mandates for broadband Internet services, whereas phone companies are required by law to share their infrastructure.[7] The lesson is, if companies are not forced to share, one can expect faster competition and service. Still, as detailed below, the open-access movement continues to push for mandatory infrastructure sharing for DSL and cable modem services.

### Open Access to Private Cable Networks

A heated national debate over forced access to cable systems developed in the late 1990s and it remains unresolved today. The debate has occasionally taken on ominous tones. Lawrence Lessig[8] has argued that we face the following choice regarding the future of broadband systems:

> Two models of network design have governed telecommunications over the past century. One produced the Internet, the other cable TV. Under the design that gave us the Internet, control is decentralized. The network owner cannot control the content or applications that run on the network. Users choose from an almost unlimited range of content and applications. Under the design of cable TV, the network owner does control the content. It decides what shows should run. If it doesn't like ABC, it gets to remove ABC from its wires— as Time Warner in fact did . . . after an argument with Disney.[9]

But is central control of a certain network by a private firm all that worrisome? It affords no immunity from market pressures. In fact, the market did work to discipline Time Warner because the company almost immediately reinstated ABC on its cable systems in the case Lessig cites. That the market is responsive to consumer demands is the real lesson to extract from the episode. Regardless, many groups continue to fear that Time Warner's recent spat with ABC and Disney illustrates the future threat of cable network providers strong-arming program providers or ISPs into deals with which they may not be comfortable. Or, in more extreme cases, these groups fear cable network owners will cut off programmers and ISPs alto-gether—which is why calls for open access to cable systems started growing louder a few years ago.

Unlike most communications industry skirmishes, the first shots in this war were fired at the local rather than the federal level. As AT&T started its massive $140 billion cable TV systems buying spree in the late 1990s,[10] many municipal regulators began raising questions about how the new system would be regulated. Municipal regulatory authorities had traditionally held considerable power over the operation of cable systems because of the franchise service territories and permits they granted to cable operators on an exclu-sive basis. In exchange, cable companies had to serve everyone in that territory, carry certain required local programming, and often submit to a variety of price controls.

Fearing that AT&T's purchase and combination of many smaller cable systems would result in a broadband monopoly in their cities, officials in San Francisco;[11] Broward County[12] and Miami–Dade County, Florida;[13] Fairfax, Virginia; St. Louis;[14] Cambridge, Massa-chusetts;[15] and Denver, Colorado, all followed the lead of Portland, Oregon, which was the first city to investigate the possibility of forcing AT&T to open its cable systems to competitors.[16] Although most of these cities eventually abandoned their crusade, Portland officials pressed the case for forced access by demanding that AT&T open its local cable system to competing ISPs at a city-determined price.

Despite its vociferous support of forced-access mandates on local telephone providers, AT&T launched a powerfully worded public relations campaign against forced access in general. As AT&T Chair-man and CEO Michael Armstrong argued in November 1998 in a speech before the Washington Metropolitan Cable Club, "No com-pany will invest billions of dollars to become a facilities-based broad-band service provider if competitors who have not invested a penny of capital nor taken an ounce of risk can come along and get a free ride on the investments and risks of others."[17] AT&T then took the city of Portland to court, saying that when it comes to new Internet technology, the market, not regulators, should determine what con-stitutes reasonable service and a fair price.

The case was litigated and eventually resolved in AT&T's favor when the U.S. Court of Appeals for the Ninth Circuit on June 22,

2000, ruled[18] that local government could not force AT&T to open its cable systems against their will.[19] It is important to note, however, that while the Ninth Circuit gave AT&T a clear victory over state and local regulators, it also suggested that cable should be reclassified as a "communications service" and regulated by the FCC accordingly.[20] In doing so, the court set the stage for the FCC to apply a common carrier model of regulation on AT&T from the federal level, which would mean open-access mandates would be applied.

*A Different Course at the FCC*

While the forced-access drama was unfolding at the local level, the FCC and then-Chairman William Kennard were charting a surprisingly different course on the issue. After spending three years engaged in a vigorous open-access campaign against local telecom companies, the FCC and Chairman Kennard argued vociferously against the imposition of forced-access mandates on cable systems by municipalities or the federal government.[21]

Kennard's rationale for treating cable differently was twofold.[22] First, Kennard argued for a "national broadband policy" with the FCC in the driver's seat.[23] Kennard stressed the need for policy uniformity as his prime justification for such a preemption of state and local authorities. "There are 30,000 local franchises in the United States. If each one decided on their own to develop technology standards for two-way communications on the cable infrastructure, there would be chaos," Kennard said.[24] Secondly, Kennard adopted a quasi–infant industry argument for keeping cable free of forced-access rules, in large part due to his desire to ensure that cable systems could present a legitimate potential alternative to the Baby Bells. In a speech before the National Cable Television Association in June of 1999, Kennard noted, "The FCC . . . has the authority to set [a national broadband policy], and we have. We have taken a deregulatory approach, an approach that will let this nascent industry flourish."[25] So local preemption and an urge to encourage competition with the Bells drove the FCC's rejection of forced access for cable systems.

However, to appease the proponents of forced access, the FCC opened a proceeding in September of 2000 entitled "Inquiry Concerning High-Speed Access to the Internet Over Cable and Other Facilities."[26] The proceeding raised the question of how to define and regulate cable-provided broadband offerings in the future and whether forced-access mandates should be applied. Finally, on March 14, 2002, the agency ruled that cable modem service would henceforth be considered an "information service" that would be free of state and local forced-access mandates and regulated under Title 1 of the Communications Act. The FCC held, "We seek to create a rational framework for the regulation of competing services that are provided via different technologies and network architectures." The commission noted that the broadband market is "evolving over multiple electronic platforms," and, therefore, the agency will "strive to develop an analytical approach that is, to the extent possible, consistent across multiple platforms." As discussed below, this is important because it set the stage for a similar ruling in the similar proceeding for teleco-provided DSL service.[27]

### The Continuing Crusade

Dozens of groups, especially ISPs, continue to push the FCC to apply open access to cable just as the agency had done for telecommunications companies in implementing the Telecom Act. In fact, after the FCC's March 2002 ruling reclassifying cable modem service as an interstate information service, a number of groups immediately filed suit, again in the Ninth Circuit Court of Appeals.[28]

The theoretical basis for this—as it was with local telecom markets—continues to be the claim that forced access would give consumers more choice and ensure "openness" on the Internet. For example, echoing Lawrence Lessig's apocalyptic warnings,[29] Andrew Jay Schwartzman of the Media Access Project said the FCC was "allowing a system that permits restrictions on where you can go and what information you can access."[30] Aside from the fact that once you're on the Internet you're on the Internet, regardless of the ISP, the notion that the government is "allowing restrictions" reflects an entirely different interpretation of what it means when a free society recognizes property rights, as if the owners of property are not the ones whose say counts. Similarly hyperbolic, the Center for Digital Democracy's Jeff Chester claimed the FCC had "struck a deadly blow to the future health of the Internet."[31] And even Internet pioneer and WorldCom senior vice president Vinton Cerf has repeatedly called for across-the-board open access,[32] urging "regulators at all levels" to "be most wary," since "Regulators and consumers are at a crossroads. One path leads to an open, competitive Internet. The other leads to an Internet whose users are locked into closed, proprietary networks by a handful of operators."[33] Ironically, Cerf's own company, WorldCom, would later have its proposed merger with Sprint halted because of similar claims.[34] That merger, however, would have been precisely the kind of offset capable of counterbalancing cable consolidation.

Again, consistency has not been a hallmark of the business community when it comes to advocating regulation. Regulation that burdens rivals is often readily supported. In a notable instance, America Online demanded open access to AT&T's cable lines to provide Internet service, only to reverse course[35] once it became a major cable provider through its merger with Time Warner in 2000. The same demand for access was made by some consumer groups,[36] particularly the OpenNet Coalition of which AOL was a member.[37] AOL's unfortunate calculation, which it regrettably led many others to adopt, was that the mere fact that it provided online service somehow gave it the right to use cable infrastructure that it played no part in helping to build or install. AOL's proper response was to use its vast resources to either buy one or more cable companies or cut legitimate deals with cable companies for access instead of asking government to shoehorn them in. Of course, that is what the company in fact ultimately did with its purchase of Time Warner.

As expected, once AOL experienced a change of heart, the forced-access community turned its attention to demanding open access to AOL's new systems and subscriber base. As Elizabeth Wasserman noted at the time, "From Disney to EarthLink to Bell South, an all-star list of enemies has come together to fight the merger of AOL and Time Warner."[38] Although the merger was not stopped outright by regulators, the Federal Trade Commission mandated that AOL offer access to its lines to competing ISPs.[39] That policy saved some rivals from the need to devise offsetting deals, and in that sense reduced competition, properly understood.

Some ISPs have continued to condemn cable's closed, proprietary nature, as if the mere fact that they were in the dial-up Internet access business bestowed a right to access the next-generation infrastructure of others. MindSpring Enterprises, Inc., CEO Charles Brewer said, "The cable industry runs a closed network. . . . That's totally unacceptable."[40] Nonetheless, apart from the AOL Time Warner consent decree, open access by ISPs to cable systems has not yet been imposed as a general policy. And most cable operators are naturally migrating toward voluntary access plans because it makes good business sense for them to open their lines to others. As Dave McClure of the U.S. Internet Industry Association (which represents over 300 ISPs) noted in a recent *Los Angeles Times* article, "Granted, we have seen a move by some cable companies to shield their networks from competition. But they can't deploy broadband quick enough all by themselves. They are going to need to fill their networks with other Internet service providers."[41] The same article quoted technology analyst and former FCC chief of staff Blair Levin. "The cable operators have figured out that having multiple ISPs helps bring traffic on their network, and they make money when there is traffic on their network."[42] Those reactions confirm the marketplace principle that competitive pressures come from all market participants; the reality is that each player needs the others and there is no cause to fear the free market.

Even if some cable operators chose not to open their systems to rivals, it would not justify forced-access regulation. Indeed, cable operators, and all broadband network owners for that matter, need to have control over their systems if they ever hope to attract the investment needed to build them in the first place. As *Wall Street Journal* business columnist Holman W. Jenkins Jr. noted in a September 2000 editorial presciently titled "How a Telecom Meltdown Will Cause the Next Recession," "Growth in the economy is not the product of the extracurricular activities of the tooth fairy. In our economy, it comes from the huge confidence ... of investors that they will be able to realize the wealth-generating potential of the new digital technologies."[43] Furthermore, as Jenkins put it in another column, "Allowing companies to reap the full reward of their investment would be a spur to others to invest to create alternative delivery networks."[44] Similarly, Douglas S. Shapiro of Deutsche Bank Securities warned in 1998:

> Forcing cable operators to unbundle would essentially send the following message to anyone seeking to build an advanced communications system: go ahead and build the network under the presumption you'll be able to realize returns commensurate with the risk, but we'll step in right before you're able to realize that return and force you to open your network to all competitors. As a result, it could signal the

death knell for any number of other proposed, but unbuilt, high-bandwidth communications systems, such as very high frequency satellite services (like Teledesic or Spaceway), or those built by electric utilities, broadcasters, and cable over-builders, among others.[45]

And imposing common carriage mandates on cable systems would not be nearly as simple as some claim. As FCC Chairman Michael Powell argued at the October 2001 "National Summit on Broadband Deployment":

> When someone advocates regulatory regimes for broadband that look like, smell like, feel like common carriage, scream at them! They will almost always suggest it is just a "light touch." Demand to see the size of the hand that is going to lay its finger on the market. Insist on knowing where it all stops. Require they explain who gets to make the key decisions—if it is enlightened regulators, rather than consumers and producers, walk out of the meeting.[46]

Chairman Powell's comments wisely raise concerns about the difficulty of imposing forced-access mandates in a complex and fast-paced sector. "In practice, governments are not omniscient. They are almost always at an informational disadvantage compared with the parties that they are trying to influence . . . ," notes Lawrence J. White of New York University.[47] Forced-access regulation of cable networks would be especially difficult in light of the industry's complicated architecture. Having not been designed for broadband data delivery, most cable is not yet ready for two-way traffic; indeed, examination of the infrastructure has shown that nearly all of it would require replacement to make it ready.[48] Such upgrades are extremely expensive, and mandatory access proposals kill incentives to do even those upgrades, let alone the incentives of cable companies to form fiber partnerships to enable the next-level Internet. As David Kopel of the Heartland Institute notes, "The technology to accommodate forced access does not presently exist,"[49] and it is simply not feasible for cable operators to open their systems to every rival that wants space on the carrier's network.[50]

Finally, Thomas W. Hazlett of the American Enterprise Institute and George Bittlingmayer of the University of Kansas have shown that there are important and unappreciated benefits to allowing proprietary control of cable broadband networks:

> The categorical argument that networks limiting access reduce social welfare is demonstrably false. Some benefits flow from the creation of open environments, but benefits may also be created in solutions limiting access to one degree or another. The set of trade-offs is large, their evaluation complex. Optimizing social value requires a mix that recognizes where openness is appropriate and where proprietary restrictions make sense. A simple rule forbidding all but entirely open systems would damage consumers by dramatically reducing both infrastructure investment and Internet functionality.[51]

The debate is far from over. Congress has considered legislation on this front before and may do so again. Some policymakers still hope to generalize the requirements imposed on AOL Time Warner's cable systems. Rep. Rick Boucher (D-Va.) plans to reintroduce an open-access bill for cable broadband requiring that operators open their lines to rival ISPs, calling it "still necessary, perhaps more necessary than ever."[52] And numerous advocates of forced access, including now the American Civil Liberties Union,[53] are stepping up their efforts to impose forced access through either Congress, the courts, or various regulatory agencies.[54] So the debate over forced access to cable broadband networks is really just beginning.

### Open Access to DSL Internet Service

Unlike the cable broadband market, which is threatened with forced-access mandates but has so far not succumbed to them (except as a condition of merger approval in the case of AOL Time Warner), the local carrier market mandates requiring infrastructure sharing are routinely imposed on the broadband services provided by incumbent ILECs. The twisted-pair copper wires to the home that transmit telephone calls can also transmit high-speed Internet service with appropriate upgrades through DSL service. As summarized above, regulators already mandate interconnection, unbundling, and line sharing for the ILECs, and they have argued that these rules can be extended so that rivals (resellers) can also provide Internet service to customers. As Robert Crandall has summarized:

> Many of us have heard that the government wants to keep its hands off the Internet. Yet today telephone companies cannot compete in high-speed Internet access without complying with an intricate set of rules that do not apply to cable

companies or even wireless carriers. They have to offer new services, such as DSL, from a separate subsidiary or under state-regulated rates. They have to share their lines with any prospective competitor and often at very low rates. And if the new DSL services prove to be profitable, the telephone companies may be forced by state regulators to cut their other rates.[55]

In August 1998, almost exactly two years to the day after the FCC released its famous Local Competition Order[56] establishing forced-access guidelines for local voice services, the agency promulgated its Advanced Services Order,[57] which advocated the extension of unbundling rules to high-speed Internet and data services provided by the ILECs.[58] The FCC held that the open-access provisions found in section 251 of the Telecom Act should "apply equally to advanced services and to circuit-switched voice services." Moreover, "incumbent LECs are subject to the interconnection obligations . . . with respect to both their circuit-switched and packet-switched networks" and that "the facilities and equipment used by incumbent LECs to provide advanced services are network elements and subject to the [network sharing] obligations." The order further noted:

> Thus, for example, all incumbent LECs must provide requesting telecommunications carriers with unbundled loops capable of transporting high-speed digital signals, and must offer unbundled access to the equipment used in the provision of advanced services, subject to considerations of technical feasibility and the provisions of section 251(d)(2). . . . However, to the extent that an incumbent LEC chooses to establish an affiliate that is truly separate from the incumbent to provide these advanced services, that affiliate would not be an incumbent LEC under the Act, and would therefore not be subject to incumbent LEC regulation.[59]

### A Nonlevel Regulatory Playing Field

The 1998 Advanced Services Order continues to be hotly debated at the FCC, in Congress, and in the courts, especially as the Bells ponder the deployment of truly "advanced" broadband networks and technologies that don't necessarily ride on top of their existing systems. But the FCC's actions beg an even more practical question about the regulation of broadband in the future: If various companies from formerly distinct industry sectors (teleco, cable, wireless) are now all attempting to provide similar types of service (high-speed broadband access), should not they be regulated on equal terms by government officials? Unfortunately, they are not treated equally today.

P. H. Longstaff notes that "our business and regulatory strategies are often tied to a specific technology. But separate strategies for each may soon be difficult to justify. Broadcasting, telephone, cable, and satellites are all heading in the same technological direction and competing for the same customers."[60] Likewise, Huber et al. have argued, "How telecommunications services are regulated today depends in large part on what the FCC calls them. . . . A complex regulatory taxonomy has grown up over many decades, and not surprisingly, it mirrors the distinction and lines drawn under the 1934 Communications Act."[61] What the authors are referring to is the FCC's apples-versus-oranges approach to communications industry regulation.

In today's market, few players continue to refer to themselves as "cable companies," "telephone providers," "cellular firms," or "broadcasters." The increasing reality of technological convergence means these formerly distinct industry sectors and companies are now integrating and searching for ways to offer consumers a bundled set of communications services under a single brand name. Despite that fact, FCC regulations are stuck in a regulatory time warp that lags behind current market realities by several decades. For example, the Communications Act of 1934, and subsequent statutes and regulations, carved the telecom world into administratively neat legal "titles," such as Title II (for telephony) versus Title VI (for cable services), which might have made sense in the past but do not conform to modern technological realities. And, regrettably, the Telecommunications Act of 1996 did nothing to alter the fundamental nature of these increasingly irrelevant and artificial legal distinctions.

What this means is that the FCC is currently regulating apples as apples, oranges as oranges, and bananas as bananas, when everyone is trying to provide consumers a mixed fruit salad of communications services. Again, the ultimate goal from the industry's perspective is to provide a bundled, branded commodity. In other words, provide the consumer with the full range of communications services, including voice telephony, wireless cellular, data communications, and Internet access. Asymmetrical industry regulations retard this development.

The current regulatory arrangement is indefensible because it means that firms attempting to offer comparable services are being regulated under dissimilar legal standards. It betrays a cardinal tenet of American jurisprudence—equal treatment under the law—and, from an economic point of view, could produce distorted market outcomes. Again, Huber et al. strike the right chord:

> The digital telecosm no longer conforms to these established regulatory categories, and there is no good reason to continue regulating broadband networks and services under the old regulatory paradigms. Today, voice, video, and data are converging on the same wireless and wireline networks. Step by step, regulation must be revised to reflect current technological and economic imperatives.[62]

To end the unfair system, the FCC should end this asymmetry, not by "regulating up" to put everyone on equal footing but by "deregulating down." That is, to the extent the agency continues to place ground rules on the industry at all, it should consider borrowing a page from trade law by adopting the equivalent of a "most favored nation" (MFN) clause for telecommunications. In a nutshell, this policy would state: "Any communications carrier seeking to offer a new service or entering a new line of business should be regulated no more stringently than its least regulated competitor."

MFN status for telecommunications would ensure that regulatory parity exists within the telecommunications market as the lines between existing technologies and industry sectors continue to blur. Placing everyone on the same *deregulated* level playing field should be at the heart of telecommunications policy to ensure nondiscriminatory regulatory treatment of competing providers and technologies at all levels of government.

*Signs of Change at the FCC*

The FCC is currently considering three proceedings that will offer them the opportunity to achieve the vision of a deregulated playing field.

First, as part of its "Unbundled Network Element (UNE) Triennial Review,"[63] the FCC is reexamining the list of network elements that ILECs must provide to rivals at regulated rates. As part of this massive UNE Review, the FCC is looking into the issue of whether or not it can unilaterally free the local exchange carriers from such line sharing and other unbundling requirements on their broadband services.

Second, in the "Review of Regulatory Requirements for Incumbent LEC Broadband Telecommunications Services" proceeding,[64] the agency is investigating whether the Baby Bells should be considered to hold a "dominant" position in the broadband marketplace and thus face the same pricing and infrastructure sharing rules that govern the voice market. This is important because if Bell-provided DSL is labeled a "nondominant" service, it means the Bells would be free to offer broadband services to the public without facing a host of line-sharing mandates and other open-access requirements. Since cable companies currently control roughly 70 percent of the residential broadband marketplace, it seems likely that the FCC will have no other choice but to declare Bell-provided high-speed DSL services "nondominant."

Third, on February 14, 2002, the FCC opened a proceeding that will "resolve outstanding issues regarding the classification of telephone-based broadband Internet access services and the regulatory implications of that classification."[65] This investigation is important because if telephone-provided broadband were classified as an "information service" it would mean that DSL would fall under Title I instead of Title II of the Communications Act. Title II regulations, which cover traditional wireline telephony, impose a host of common carriage requirements on companies, including price regulations, interconnection mandates, and unbundling and line-sharing rules. By comparison, services that are designated "information services" and covered under Title I face far fewer regulations. As mentioned above, a similar proceeding[66] designated cable-provided high-speed service an "information service" in March 2002, so the stage is set for a similar ruling for teleco-provided broadband services. Nonetheless, numerous companies and organizations have encouraged the FCC to take the opposite path and expand unbundling rules to DSL services.[67]

Finally, there have been ongoing efforts on Capitol Hill to address these issues. In the 107th Congress, two controversial bills proposed to clarify the law by minimizing regulation of broadband. One bill, the Internet Freedom and Broadband Deployment Act of 2001 (H.R. 1542), was sponsored by House Energy and Commerce Chairman Billy Tauzin (R-La.) and ranking minority member John Dingell (D-Mich.). The hotly debated Tauzin-Dingell bill would allow the Baby

Bell companies to provide customers with broadband services the same way cable and satellite companies are currently allowed to, largely free of infrastructure-sharing mandates. On February 27, 2002, after months of acrimonious debate, the House of Representatives finally passed a watered-down version of the bill and passed it along to the mostly unsympathetic Senate Commerce Committee, which was ruled with an iron hand by longtime Baby Bell basher Sen. Ernest Hollings (D-S.C.). Hollings and a number of his colleagues vociferously denounced the Tauzin-Dingell bill and vowed to kill the measure, or to go further and introduce legislation to actually impose new regulations on telecom and broadband markets.

Despite the generally hostile reception that the Tauzin-Dingell measure received in the Senate, a second measure—S. 2430, the Broadband Regulatory Parity Act of 2002—was introduced by Sens. John Breaux (D-La.) and Don Nickles (R-Okla.). It would demand that the FCC ensure regulatory parity among the various providers of broadband services. Importantly, the Breaux-Nickles bill would achieve this parity not by "regulating up" to put carriers on equal footing but by "deregulating down."[68] The bill states that "all providers of broadband service, and all providers of broadband access services, are subject to the same regulatory requirements, or no regulatory requirements" and requires that those provisions "are implemented without increasing the regulatory requirements applicable to any provider of broadband services."[69] Through such MFN-like provisions, the bill establishes a simple legal standard to help level the playing field in the broadband marketplace.

So, in essence, the Tauzin-Dingell and Breaux-Nickles measures propose to clarify communications law by creating a firewall between old voice-grade regulations and new broadband services and free new systems from infrastructure-sharing requirements. These debates on Capitol Hill and at the FCC are important not only because they determine how current Bell broadband offerings such as DSL are governed, but also because they will play a key role in how future services, such as fiber, are deployed by companies in the future.[70]

### Forced Access and Newer Broadband Alternatives

Cable modems and DSL are today's dominant broadband technologies, but they are not the only show in town. Numerous facilities-based alternatives are being planned or are already in place in today's market and prove that duplicating facilities is not as unthinkable as the natural monopoly theorists would have us believe. Moreover, the existence of these technologies raises important questions about whether forced-access mandates will be applied in these emerging markets.

*Fiber Optics*

Unless there is a satellite or wireless revolution, getting real data transmission speed—instant multiple media downloads and teleconferencing—will require new infrastructure like "fiber to the home" (FTTH). No one is yet proposing mandatory access to FTTH because it is far from conquering the marketplace and is extraordinarily expensive. But the open-access model applied to lesser modes of broadband can certainly delay the arrival of FTTH. Regulatory certainty is needed by would-be entrepreneurs if they are to risk their capital. They need to know that their cables and infrastructure won't be seized before they will dare extend fiber to the home on a grand scale. Mandated access to other types of broadband could easily hinder FTTH initiatives.

Data transmission speeds over fiber are far faster than the speeds provided by either cable or DSL broadband technology. Given likely future bandwidth demands, cable and DSL may prove as unacceptable as a 28K modem is today. As a result, unless there are substantial breakthroughs in wireless data transmission, a multi-billion-dollar campaign to rewire the so-called "last mile" to household consumers may materialize. Here especially, cross-industry consortia, such as cost-sharing arrangements with power entrepreneurs (now cut off from customers by local exclusive franchises), could prove essential.

If e-commerce ultimately does fulfill predictions of being a multi-trillion-dollar industry, and if potential revenues from offering multiple online services (video, telephony, music, gaming, conferencing) to the homeowner reach the level of $150 per month or so, at some point the potential returns from extending fiber start to make sense.[71] Potential future applications include receiving transmission from one's choice of dozens of high-definition cameras positioned at sporting events, increasingly sophisticated—eventually possibly even holographic—gaming over the Internet, and intensive video conferencing.[72] Instantaneous downloads and virtual reality are other potential applications. The bandwidth needed to deliver it all will be extraordinary. Consumers will be waiting for these and other new services for years longer than necessary if policymakers persist in imposing the regulated open-access model.

Some have proposed that fiber to the home may displace cable and DSL in the coming decade.[73] Getting fiber to the curb, or at least to the neighborhood, is the first step. One option is an approach called a passive optical network (PON). Because a single fiber goes to a node where it is split and can then service business parks, shopping centers, or homes, the PON may be cheaper than a separate fiber to each home. Maintenance costs are lower because unlike typical fiber systems, "Outside a central office, PON gear needs no electronics or power source." Data for 16 to 32 homes,[74] or 12 businesses, can be sent along one line and then split. (Businesses usually connect to the fiber by fast hookups like T-1.)

Part of the picture may consist of consumers installing their own hardware at home, like the plastic optical fiber, which will save vendors much of the awesome installation costs. While there is no broadband "killer application" yet (aside from mere e-mail, which was the killer app for narrowband Internet), presumably when appetites are whetted the market will expand. (Once consumers can download video instantaneously and with ease, they may want 3D holograms.)

Wireless may, of course, win the broadband race. But if not, FTTH will often mean tearing up streets again and a tremendous amount of disruption. Unfortunately, that kind of massive disruption can itself lead to calls for regulation. But on the other hand, as George Mason University professor James Trefil put it, "Any infrastructure you put in is going to be disruptive during installation ... a city whose streets aren't all torn up is on its way to death."[75]

Marred streets signal an esthetic problem and perhaps a failure to clearly define or assign property rights so that future disruption is minimized—not necessarily a natural monopoly problem that calls for open access regulation. But marred streets don't necessarily justify centrally managed mandatory access policies. Those who do dig could simply be required to restore the property to the same or better condition (in a property rights regime, that is a given). There are ways electric power companies, water companies, real estate developers, and others can help share the costs and benefits and lessen disruption. Redundant conduits can be buried so that next-generation fiber can be inserted without excavating, as companies already do with fiber installation.

### Cable "Overbuilders"

In many cities in America, so-called "overbuilders" are establishing their own facilities and network infrastructure to get around traditional communications providers.[76] These systems typically offer significant fiber-optic capacity and bundled phone, cable television, and high-speed Internet packages to square off against both cable and telephone giants.

RCN Corporation,[77] for example, is the nation's leading overbuilder and competes head-to-head with incumbents in many urban areas, including Boston, New York, Philadelphia, Chicago, Los Angeles, San Francisco, and Washington, D.C. Through its Starpower service in the Washington market, RCN has been able to capture market share from larger players and win the praise of many. The *Washington Post* recently noted that "Starpower has chipped away at Comcast's dominance, quarter after business quarter, and a choice of providers is available to about 80 percent of city residents. . . . This is, though, about much more than cable television. It's about what Starpower and the rest of the industry call bundling, which means providing consumers with several electronic gee-whiz choices through a single line from a single company."[78] And the *New York Times* reports that "RCN's mere existence carries a larger significance: It is possible for a small start-up company to challenge the local telephone behemoths and cable television incumbents and give residential consumers a choice of provider for both basic communications services and fast Internet access."[79]

Some other overbuilders include Knology[80] (serving about a dozen cities throughout the Southeast); WideOpenWest[81] (serving customers in five states); Grande Communications[82] (serving central Texas); Altrio Communications[83] (serving Southern California); and Seren Innovations/Astound[84] (serving St. Cloud, Minnesota, and expanding into other markets). Other overbuilders have fallen on hard times with the recent market downturn and a drying up of venture capital funding. However, a major difference between overbuilding today and past efforts is the existence of numerous revenue streams: while it may not have made economic sense to build a new network merely to supply cable television, these innovators offer not just video but data and telephone service as well.[85] The economics with respect to the cost of installation and the revenue that can be charged have changed, and they look better as networks become capable of providing more than just one type of "plain vanilla" service to customers. On a more simplistic note, many customers prefer having one bill for a bundled service rather than dealing with two or more providers and bills.

### Undersea Fiber

The potential problems with installing network infrastructure like power lines or fiber can seem small compared with those confronted in sinking fiber-optic cable in the oceans. While such projects and their sponsors have fallen on hard times in the recent technology downturn, the risks undertaken by private market actors provide lessons for the natural monopoly fundamentalists. Moreover, the infrastructure that has been put in place will not disappear, despite the fate of any particular company. One such project was the Fiberoptic Link around the Globe. Built by a consortium of Nynex, Cable & Wireless, and Sprint, this is a 17,000-mile cable connecting London and Japan, one of the longest engineering projects in history.[86] Another endeavor, the $14 billion, 30-partner Project Oxygen, proposed installing 199,000 miles touching 175 countries.[87] KMI Corporation president John Kessler called it "the most ambitious project of communications in the 20th century."[88] But the telecom downturn has led to these projects being built piecemeal; and rivals have started their own networks.[89] Nonetheless, the fact that such investments have been made and that rivals have initiated separate projects only reinforces the legitimacy of the principles of redundancy and facilities-based competition.

That said, even though such consortia (one might call them partial, or limited-purpose, mergers) are necessary for huge-scale networks, incumbents protest perceived monopolization. In 1999, even Global Crossing sought to have FCC regulators defer a consortium of more than 30 telecommunications firms (including MCI WorldCom, AT&T, SBC Communications, and Sprint) from setting up a separate undersea cable to compete with its own, because of the potential for monopolization.[90] Global Crossing's "petition to defer" called the consortium a "collusive system" that "would appear to harm incumbent carriers, end users and new entrants in the market."[91] Where that kind of mindset prevails, facilities-based or infrastructure competition truly has no chance.

Such networks truly are remarkable engineering feats. A *Wall Street Journal* article described the example of a Cable & Wireless fiber-laying ship called the *Innovator* that carried 2,170 miles of cable, whose line trails and touches the ocean floor 19 miles behind.[92] In shallow water, the cable must be buried with an undersea plow to avoid its being snapped by fishing trawlers.[93] Ships are now capable of installing transatlantic cables in less than two months.[94] Such projects entail negotiating with regulators around the world—not just a state public utility commission or a federal agency like the FERC. For those who speak the language, undersea fiber is a prime example of a "natural monopoly"—yet the risk rests with these companies, not their customers, as is the case with regulated utilities.

*Satellite*

Direct broadcast satellite (DBS) service is a well-known success story in the video distribution marketplace, providing serious facilities-based competition to cable and traditional broadcast services. Now DBS providers like DirecTV and EchoStar are turning their attention to broadband markets.

For example, DirecTV offers broadband service through its DirecPC system, but requires a phone connection for part of the transmission.[95] The company is developing a faster two-way system called Spaceway in partnership with others. Likewise, EchoStar offers satellite broadband through StarBand Communications in partnership with several other companies including Microsoft.[96]

An exciting new technological derivative of DBS looms with Northpoint Technology, which proposes to use the same spectrum DBS companies do to offer service but from the northern instead of the southern sky. Current DBS subscribers point their receiving dishes south to capture the signals being beamed from satellites in geosynchronous orbit around the Earth. Northpoint's "Broadwave USA" system would instead use terrestrial towers located to the north of most dish owners in America to allow the reuse of DBS spectrum and provide a serious competitive alternative to existing entertainment and broadband providers.[97]

And even more ambitious satellite ventures are under way. Wireless telecom entrepreneur Craig McCaw, for example, has helped funnel billions into satellite ventures such as New ICO and Teledesic.[98] These satellite constellations would offer ubiquitous high-speed service across the globe—a veritable "fiber optic network in outer space."[99] While the systems are elaborate and quite expensive (and it remains unclear if Teledesic will ever get off the ground),[100] they have attracted an impressive group of investors, including Microsoft founder Bill Gates.[101]

Luckily, satellite providers have not yet been threatened with broadband forced-access mandates as teleco and cable providers have, although forced-access mandates were discussed as a condition of the EchoStar-DirecTV merger agreement.[102] But a different variety of open-access rules have been imposed on the video programming side of their business in the form of "must-carry" or retransmission rules on DBS providers, which are discussed in the next chapter.

*Fixed Terrestrial Wireless and "Wi-Fi" Networks*

Despite the checkered past of the fixed wireless sector, riddled with noticeable business failures such as Teligent and Winstar,[103] many companies continue to deploy fixed terrestrial wireless networks to offer residential and business customers a wire-free last-mile solution for their communications and broadband needs.[104] Also called multichannel multipoint distribution service (MMDS), fixed wireless has traditionally depended on land-based towers that transmit line-of-sight signals to rooftop antennas. This cell phone–like configuration offers respectable territorial coverage (from 20 to 50 miles), but service can be limited by line-of-sight limitations. Additional towers can alleviate some of these problems.[105] Large carriers such as AT&T, WorldCom, and Sprint have experimented with MMDS in the past, but only Sprint continues to offer service.[106]

Although traditional fixed terrestrial wireless services have never been able to garner much market share, increasingly popular next-generation fixed wireless "wi-fi" (short for "wireless fidelity") services have the potential to capture a much greater share of the broadband marketplace.[107] This technology, which is also occasionally referred to as "802.11" after the technical standard it is based on, allows multiple users to share the same broadband connection through the use of wireless transmitter and miniature receiving devices that can be installed in laptop computers, cell phones, and many other mobile communications devices. Although it is distance-limited, within certain ranges it offers speedy broadband connectivity.[108]

As John Markoff of the *New York Times* notes,"The rapid emergence of the 802.11 standard has been a remarkable phenomenon that has so far been unplanned and moved forward largely without the backing of major corporate service providers."[109] Wi-fi networks are springing up in many airports, hotels, and coffee shops as an easy way for "on-the-go" users to engage in mobile networking.[110] Smaller wi-fi providers such as Boingo,[111] hereUare Communications,[112] SkyPilot,[113] WayPort,[114] iPass,[115] and even coffee giant Starbucks are deploying wi-fi networks across America that consumers can subscribe to for $30 to $75 per month. Starbucks currently offers wi-fi connections in 600 of their coffee shops for $30 per month and plans to expand service to 4,000 stores by the end of 2003.[116] Only recently have larger companies begun to get involved. For example, the *New York Times* reported in mid-July 2002 that Intel, IBM, AT&T Wireless, Verizon Communications, and Cingular were considering a joint effort to deploy wi-fi networks across America.[117]

Some informal groups take a more aggressive bottom-up approach to wi-fi deployment by encouraging large communities of users to share network capacity by establishing a link to existing broadband systems and then allowing numerous users to tap into it free of charge.[118] This makes some established cable and teleco carriers nervous because subscribers using a single broadband hookup might then allow hundreds or thousands of other users to tap into the network through wi-fi connections. Some carriers such as AOL Time Warner and AT&T Broadband appear to be taking the threat seriously: they are attempting to crack down on subscribers that share their network connection with large groups.[119] While these companies are legitimately worried about wi-fi users putting too much demand on the system, it is likely that innovative business plans will be worked out in the future to accommodate such growth. For example, metered billing might quickly solve the problem by charging subscribers for the amount of traffic they are bringing to a network. Although pay-as-you-go metered billing is quite unpopular with a public accustomed to all-you-can-eat flat rate pricing plans for Internet access, it may be one of many solutions companies will try to use to ensure costs are fairly allocated for network usage.

Once such issues are worked out, the future looks bright for some form of wi-fi broadband, especially since it remains unregulated by the FCC[120] Indeed, former FCC chairman Reed Hundt has boldly proclaimed that wi-fi could lead to a "broadband nirvana" if regulators do not get in the way of its development.[121]

*Ultra-Wideband and Free Space Optics*

These emerging technologies promise to take the world into a Star Trek-esque age of wireless information networking. Ultra-wideband (UWB) "operates by releasing many small bursts of radio signals over a wide swath of radio spectrum, in contrast to more established wireless technologies, which issue a protracted signal over a limited frequency range," explains Matt Carolan in *EWeek* magazine.[122] *The Economist* further clarifies the technology: "Rather than transmitting and receiving on a particular radio frequency, [UWB] involves transmitting very short pulses on a wide range of frequencies simultaneously at low power. Such pulses, which are typically less than a billionth of a second long, pass unnoticed by conventional radio receivers, but can be detected by a UWB receiver."[123]

Because it can coexist within the radio spectrum with many other overlapping services and technologies, UWB "creates a new model for regulation because it can allow multiple use of the same spectrum," argues Edmond J. Thomas, chief of the FCC's Office of Engineering and Technology.[124] In other words, UWB can help squeeze much more capacity out of existing spectrum. The real advantage of UWB over alternative wireless technologies is that given the "spread spectrum" physics behind it, UWB has "an inherent ability to maintain high speed through walls and in cluttered high-multipath environments."[125] But the technology is currently distance-limited and will probably be used for short-haul wireless networking applications.

On February 14, 2002, UWB technologies received a formal blessing from the FCC when the agency ruled that the technology could be freely developed within certain confines so long as it did not interfere with existing spectrum technologies.[126] Companies such as Xtreme Spectrum[127] and Time Domain Corporation[128] are working to deploy UWB systems today.

By comparison, free space optics (FSO) uses low-power infrared lasers to offer consumers fiber optic–quality data connections without the fiber.[129] Firms such as TeraBeam,[130] AirFiber,[131] and Light-Point[132] propose to connect consumers to the laser light networks via transmitting equipment in the office or home, offering data services with "no dialing, no modems, no traveling through underground passageways."[133] While they do require direct line of sight or leapfrogging from building to building, proponents of FSO claim "lasers do not require costly wireless spectrum licenses, access to rooftop rights-of-way, or trenches under city streets."[134] Moreover, "With sunk costs well below those of rival broadband technologies, FSO companies offer last-mile connectivity at a fraction of competitors' prices," notes Brian E. Taptich in *Red Herring* magazine.[135] He concludes, "There are none of the laborious, bureaucratic delays associated with laying new fiber [all the way to the home or business]."[136]

Such companies have ample incentives to make revenue-sharing deals with property owners and landlords to site the equipment. But while FSO technology is currently unregulated by the FCC, regulation may rear its head here, too, through the technology's connection to buildings and landlords, given that regulators have considered requiring landlords to allow access to office building rooftops and internal wiring conduits, an idea that property owners vehemently reject.[137] Just as broadband companies should not be subjected to access requirements, neither should they get special favors from legislators.[138] Nevertheless, one hopes this will not lead to full-blown regulation of FSO because the technology offers real promise in terms of future competition. As Anthony Acampora, professor of electrical and computer engineering at the University of California, San Diego, wrote in the June 17, 2002, online edition of *Scientific American*, "Although free-space optics has some distance to go in addressing its remaining concerns, it's still the best bet to reach across the last mile and bring about the long-awaited broadband revolution."[139]

### A Bold Broadband Future?

The point of the preceding technological showcase was not to endorse any particular broadband service but to point out that many alternative broadband technologies are on the proverbial drawing board, or even currently at work in today's marketplace. Many of these business ventures will fail and many of the technologies will not pan out. But some form of broadband will succeed, and the very fact that entrepreneurs are engaged in such ventures serves as powerful testimony to the ability of the market to respond to consumer needs without regulatory intervention.

Open-access proposals would threaten to halt critical developments by such entrepreneurs to bridge the last mile to consumers' homes. Few will install fiber or deploy sophisticated wireless solutions for broadband Internet tomorrow if forced access is a precedent on today's lesser delivery options. People want multiple phones; they want instant downloads of video and sound; they want an always-on Internet. Entrepreneurs could provide all this and more, but they won't if they are simply granted access to the wires that exist.

Rejection of the natural monopoly model in favor of competition in the creation of redundant, overlapping, proprietary but ultrafast broadband networks is just as important as competition in the goods, services, and content sold over those networks. Open-access models, in seeking the second, can kill the possibility for the first. The bandwidth we really need would probably best emerge over many years as the product of cross-industry consortia among many network industries, but it won't happen if all the potential players simply ride on the existing networks, as is the trend today. Besides, markets have natural tendencies toward open access, and it need not be forced by a regulator: as the market for broadband service grows and network companies seek to expand to new regions, those companies will have to offer open access in their own regions. Such reciprocation likely means that open access may be the standard model anyway, but on a voluntarily negotiated basis, without the mandates that can restrict next-generation technology.

# 7. Case Study 4: Must-Carry Mandates on Cable and Satellite Networks

Must-carry rules present a different, but equally destructive, form of forced-access regulation. In this case, mandatory access rules are intended to offer America's local broadcast television stations free channel capacity on private cable and satellite networks. These mandates dictate that every local TV station—including less popular UHF channels—be given a free ride on the infrastructure owned and operated by their cable and satellite competitors. As with other industries and technologies, forced access in this case has also created unintended consequences and done more to hinder than to foster the development of true competition.

## The Cable Industry, Retransmission Consent, and Must-Carry Mandates

Before discussing the specific problems associated with must-carry regulation, it is important to understand that cable industry carriage policy has two important components: must-carry mandates and retransmission consent. Retransmission consent deals with the right of cable companies (and later satellite carriers) to rebroadcast the signal and content provided by licensed broadcast television stations. Retransmission consent is complex because it involves both a copyright component and a broadcast signal retransmission component, both of which are regulated under a separate set of legal standards.[1]

While the cable industry has been fighting federal efforts to impose must-carry mandates for more than 30 years, they have also been fighting for the right to retransmit broadcast signals to the public. Indeed, in the early days of cable, this was the core business model for the industry: retransmitting existing broadcast signals to consumers and communities with poor over-the-air reception. So the preservation of their retransmission rights has always been an important objective for cable.

For this reason, it is likely that retransmission consent agreements would have been struck naturally between broadcasters and cable networks even in an unregulated environment. In a hypothetical free market for video programming, broadcasters and television programmers would have fought cable companies over the right to control the distribution of their programming. In all likelihood, contracts eventually would have been negotiated between these parties because each side had something to gain by offering the public wider program distribution. Of course, no such free market in video programming existed as these issues were coming to the fore, so regulators arbitrarily decided on what they thought was the best arrangement at the time.

On the copyright front, the cable industry initially won the right to retransmit without being forced to deal with copyright issues,[2] but during a revision of copyright law by Congress in 1976, a compulsory licensing scheme was created that forced cable operators to pay copyright holders according to a complex formula. However, since Congress only dealt with the copyright part of the retransmission equation at that time, oversight for retransmission of the actual broadcast signal still fell to the FCC.

The FCC's early attempts to deal with these matters in the 1960s and 1970s were largely focused on protecting broadcast interests. Regulators have been committed to preserving free, over-the-air television broadcasting since its inception, and anything thought to be a potential threat to it has been viewed with apprehension and thus strictly regulated. In an effort to shield broadcasters from the potential rising threat of cable competition during this time, the FCC implemented rules outlining what cable firms could and could not transmit to the public. The regulations that the FCC promulgated included must-carry regulations that required cable operators to retransmit the signals of local broadcasters on their networks in an effort to ensure that no local broadcaster would be threatened by competition from distant signals or other independent channels that cable operators offered on their systems.

These must-carry rules were opposed by the cable industry and subsequently challenged in court. In the 1985 case *Quincy Cable TV, Inc. v. FCC*,[3] the District of Columbia Circuit Court struck down these mandates as a violation of the cable industry's First Amendment rights. Undeterred, the FCC issued a revised set of must-carry rules in an attempt to pass muster with the courts. These new regulations exempted smaller cable carriers from must-carry requirements but demanded that larger operators commit 25 percent of their total channel capacity to retransmission of local broadcast signals. Despite the small-carrier exemption the revised rules were once again struck down by the D.C. Circuit Court two years later in *Century Communications Corp. v. FCC*.[4]

After two failed attempts to impose must-carry through regulatory fiat, broadcasters turned their attention to Congress and successfully pushed for the inclusion of similar mandates as part of the Cable Television Consumer Protection and Competition Act of 1992, or the "Cable Act of 1992." Under the Cable Act, which was passed over the veto of the elder President Bush, Congress did what the FCC had been blocked from doing by the courts for several years: require cable companies to carry the signals of local television broadcasters without being compensated for doing so. Mimicking the provisions of the FCC's earlier must-carry rules, the Cable Act required very small cable carriers (those with less than 12 channels) to carry only 3 broadcast channels, but any cable company with more than 12 channels was forced to devote one-third of their channel capacity to must-carry.

Retransmission consent was also an important component of the Cable Act. In fact, the Cable Act gave broadcasters the choice of opting to fall under must-carry for their station or attempting to negotiate retransmission rights with the cable operators. In subsequent years, most larger broadcasters have chosen the model of negotiated consent, but many smaller stations have opted to exercise their must-carry powers under the law.

The new must-carry rules were once again challenged by the cable industry, but the resulting 1994 Supreme Court decision in *Turner Broadcasting System, Inc. v. FCC*[5] was decided against industry this time, albeit by a narrow 5 to 4 majority. Although the Court found that cable operators did indeed deserve *some* level of First Amendment protection from government interference, the slim majority ruled that cable did not deserve the same strict level of First Amendment scrutiny that other forms of media (like newspapers) were granted. Thus, using this strange and quite indefensible standard,[6] the Court reasoned that must-carry was constitutional and the Cable Act rules could stand. When the Supreme Court had a chance to revisit the rules in 1997 in *Turner Broadcasting System, Inc v. FCC*,[7] or "*Turner* II" as it is more commonly called, the Court once again upheld the constitutionality of the must-carry mandates using similar logic. Inexplicably, the cable industry did not employ a Fifth Amendment "takings" defense in these cases but instead hoped to win on First Amendment grounds alone.

### Making a Bad Situation Worse: Dual Must-Carry

Shortly after the Court's *Turner* II ruling, the FCC initiated its *Notice of Proposed Rulemaking in the Matter of Carriage of Digital Television Broadcast Signals*,[8] which posed the question of whether must-carry mandates should be extended to cover the retransmission of digital television (DTV) signals. With the Supreme Court ruling in their favor in *Turner* I and *Turner* II, TV broadcasters decided to up the ante by encouraging policymakers to mandate that cable providers be forced to retransmit the broadcast industry's digital channels in addition to older analog signals. This is commonly referred to as dual must-carry or "multiple must-carry" regulation.

By way of background, in 1996, every broadcast television station in America was granted a second 6-megahertz (MHz) television license over which they would be allowed to make the transition to high-definition digital television (HDTV). Broadcasters argued that they would need this second slice of spectrum to simulcast digital signals alongside analog broadcasts until Americans made the complete transition to DTV sets. Once everyone has converted to digital sets, broadcasters promise to return the old analog spectrum to the FCC for reauction. In the meantime, however, the broadcasters did not want to pay for their new digital spectrum, which was quite valuable "beach front quality" spectrum. Estimates of the value of the spectrum given to the broadcasters to make the transition to DTV ranged from $10 billion to $100 billion. The logic behind this giveaway was that local over-the-air broadcasting remained an important public service that should be continued in the digital age regardless of cost.

Amazingly, as part of the Telecom Act of 1996, broadcasters convinced policymakers to execute this plan. Broadcaster license holders were "loaned" an additional license free of charge even though many other spectrum users were salivating at the prospect of bidding billions to obtain that same spectrum for other uses. The broadcasters later won a very important concession from Congress: they would continue to transmit analog signals on their old 6-MHz analog slice of spectrum until 2006, *or until 85 percent of Americans had made the DTV transition,* and only then return the old spectrum to the FCC for reauction.

Unfortunately, the transition is not going well.[9] In fact, the industrial policy might derail entirely. Only a small percentage of American homes currently have DTV. Because of the limited selection of over-the-air broadcast digital programming available, consumers have not felt the need to make the expensive switch. Thus, the 2006 deadline will certainly be missed, and the transition will continue indefinitely until Americans find a compelling reason to make the move to DTV.[10]

This has important ramifications for the question of dual or multiple must-carry for cable systems. If the broadcasters have no foreseeable chance of making the successful transition to DTV, how long should cable companies be expected to carry both the analog and digital versions of a broadcaster's programming? With cable operators already strapped with analog must-carry mandates that eat up capacity and offer them no compensation in return, the addition of even more bandwidth-intensive digital must-carry channels would begin to seriously compromise their ability to carry the other channels or services they want, including broadband Internet access. In turn, this raises the question of whether regulators will act to extend forced-access mandates to the broadband Internet offerings made by cable providers using the same logic they have employed in must-carry proceedings.[11]

### Opportunity Costs of Must-Carry

Must-carry rules are essentially corporate welfare for the broadcast sector. Using their impressive lobbying muscle, television broadcasters have convinced lawmakers that cable firms should be forced to grant space on their already crowded systems to local television stations. Regulators like to pretend that must-carry rules are the ultimate free lunch; broadcasters get to air their programming to a larger audience and cable companies get hotly demanded local news, weather, and sports as well as the popular programming that broadcast affiliates offer.

But if the public so eagerly demands local broadcast programming—and there is good evidence that they do—then cable and satellite firms will want to negotiate voluntarily with broadcasters for retransmission rights. Of course, most Americans can still put an antenna on their rooftop if they want to receive broadcast signals not carried by a cable or satellite company, but the vast majority of consumers now prefer to receive their video programming as part of a bundled subscription-based cable or satellite service package, especially because of the higher quality of the channels being retransmitted. But must-carry remains popular with many broadcasters—especially smaller stations—because it protects them from outside competition and guarantees that even the most unpopular television stations will be carried by cable and satellite companies.[12] In essence, it gives broadcasters a property right in a certain amount of the channel capacity provided by cable and satellite systems.

Must-carry rules also force unnatural trade-offs on cable companies by requiring them to substitute one type of programming for another regardless of what consumers actually demand. Consequently, some new and popular channels may be unable to find elbow room on cable systems crowded with some local channels that many consumers do not demand. While channel capacity on cable systems has expanded in recent years as carriers have upgraded to digital systems, carriage requirements will still force them to make unnatural trade-offs, especially if policymakers end up mandating "dual must-carry."

The economic trade-offs inherent in must-carry mandates should have been obvious to policymakers but apparently were not when they implemented the rules. "No one even paused to consider the [cable] spectrum was supposedly in scarce supply and that the must-carry rules gobbled up a large share of new wireline capacity," notes Peter Huber.[13] And Thomas Hazlett argues:

> Must-carry rules, by reassigning cable systems channel rights away from the party investing in the communications infrastructure, taxes channel *creation*. Because some of the conduit will not be available to carry an optimal array of revenue-producing programs, returns will be lowered. This reduces investors' incentive to invest in construction or technical upgrade enhancing capacity and, in turn, total transmissions capability (measured in program units) over time.[14]

So, once again, economists have found that forced-access mandates deter investment, innovation, and true competition. Despite such criticisms of must-carry, this form of forced-access regulation remains in place for cable operators and has recently been extended to satellite carriers as well.

### The Satellite Industry and Must-Carry Mandates

Certain provisions of the Satellite Home Viewer Improvement Act of 1999 and subsequent FCC rules[15] deal with "local-to-local" retransmission of broadcast television signals and require a DBS provider to retransmit all local television stations available within their local market if they choose to broadcast any of them at all.[16] Like cable companies, satellite providers must do so without compensation for carriage. Unlike cable providers, however, satellite providers at least have the choice of whether or not they want to retransmit any signals in the first place. Nonetheless, the "all-or-nothing" requirement under the 1999 Act essentially embodies a de facto must-carry mandate, since satellite providers want some local channels on the systems to compete against cable but must accept retransmission of all local signals as the cost of that bargain. More recently, political pressure has been brought to bear on potential DBS merger partners EchoStar and DirecTV, who have pledged to accept legally binding language committing them to transmitting local television signals into homes at a nationwide rate.[17]

The better approach here would be to free satellite and cable companies from any sort of must-carry mandates and instead allow them to negotiate voluntarily with individual broadcasters or network programmers for retransmission rights. An infrastructure already exists to provide free broadcast television. Just because that technology is bypassed and may be made obsolete by new digital satellite or cable systems does not give broadcasters the right to special treatment by a competing network. Providing space for the freeloader isn't free, and it limits alternative uses for the satellite spectrum, such as high-definition programming or broadband Internet services. Must-carry mandates should be phased out on the most rapid timetable possible.

# 8. Case Study 5: Open Access to Software

The most prominent example of "open access" in the computer software sector is none other than the case of Microsoft and the access sought by competitors to the desktop and to the operating system itself. One proposed remedy in the Microsoft case was to force the company to share code for its products,[1] or to somehow force Microsoft to create a stripped-down version of Windows that would be naturally less dominant. Although this form of access regulation isn't the same as mandating access to wire networks, the goal is the same: to undercut a rival by being granted access to its technology, infrastructure, or resources on involuntary terms. Here again, regulation threatens technology upgrades. For example, Sen. Charles Schumer (D-N.Y.) sought to urge state attorneys general to block the release of Windows XP if Microsoft did not meet conditions for providing "open access for competitors like Kodak and Real Player to offer their products on an equal basis with Microsoft products."[2]

If competitors succeed in prying open Microsoft's operating system by deeming it a sort of essential facility, the same fate could easily befall other sectors of the software industry. America Online dominates Internet access; Yahoo is a dominant portal; eBay is the dominant auction site (and has already faced competitors' calls for access to its auction listings). Even the Internet search engine Google has been deemed an essential facility by some.

Clearly the open-access mindset is on the verge of carrying over to new innovations, such as software, that have little history of natural monopoly, dominance, or even difficulty in duplication. Consider, for example, the recent case of America Online's free and popular AOL Instant Messenger (AIM) chat tool, which allows real-time, faster–than–e-mail communication. Mainly used by flirting teens, it is seen by some as presaging the future of Internet communications. *The Economist* argued, with respect to America Online's instant messaging service, as follows:

> The antitrust enforcers clearly ought to make approval of
> the AOL/Time Warner deal contingent on a cast-iron agree-
> ment to open up the merged firm's instant messaging service
> and cable networks. The success of the Internet has shown
> the value of open standards and a neutral platform on which
> everybody can compete on equal terms. Had the Internet
> been dominated by any one company, it would not be where
> it is today.[3]

AOL's dominance in messaging also bothered FCC staffers and
rivals like Microsoft and Yahoo, to whom "competition" meant lots
of players sharing the dominant party's network, rather than rivalry
that leads to emergence of a dominant system in the first place.
They called AOL a monopoly and demanded that AOL make AIM
"interoperable" with their competing IM tools, under the theory
that messaging tools should allow direct communication regardless
of provider, the way e-mail or the telephone does.

But the real display of monopolistic and anticompetitive behavior
with respect to AIM is collusion between rivals and regulators at
the FCC. AOL competitors including Yahoo, Microsoft, AT&T, and
Excite@Home formed a coalition called IMUnified to signify their
intent to develop technical interoperability standards by which all
their members will abide. Even Bill Gates telephoned FCC officials
to plead the case for "interoperability,"[4] which is puzzling since it
undercuts his own arguments against forcing Microsoft to open up
its operating system or bundle competitors' products with Windows.

However, Microsoft and Yahoo "hacked" their way into AOL's
system several times in 1999 to allow MSN Messenger and Yahoo
Messenger users to communicate with IM users. AOL blocked them.
More recently it blocked a messaging service called Trillian that was
designed to allow communication across several IM services.[5] That
must mean coalition members believe satisfactory interoperability
capabilities already exist. Yet IMUnified members are not yet even
officially interoperable with one another. They would not be interoperable at all but for the rogue efforts of a few software offerings like
OMNI that boast access to AIM and other messengers and allow
file searches across computers logged into the Napster and Gnu-
tella networks.[6]

If the coalition were to demonstrate that interoperability works
among its members and is genuinely superior, AOL's refusal to

participate would backfire as users embraced the superior new standard. (Downloading of messaging software remains free, after all.) The IMUnified coalition's failure to follow its own script indicates it isn't interested as much in an interoperability standard it as is in being handed AOL's customer base on a regulatory silver platter. The IMUnified effort is best understood as an attempt to mislead the public and to humiliate America Online.

Disregarded in the posturing about standards is the fact that AOL has already *established* a standard and needs no further validation other than that already granted it by the choices of AIM downloaders. Only that, not the desires of competitors, is relevant. AOL is in no way obliged to help other messenger services succeed. The FCC should recognize that shoehorning competitors into AOL's system is counterproductive for competition. Competing network business models are a virtue because consumer benefits depend on battles that distinguish networks from one another.

Such distinctions are emerging. MSN Messenger, for example, sports worldwide phone-calling capability. Some companies that think "business chat" represents the future have aggressive plans to use IM for real-time customer service, workforce management, and document and file sharing. Others think peer-to-peer messaging that bypasses central servers will dominate. And some note that today's chat systems are loaded with security problems and need a lot of work. If such security concerns are genuine, then forcing everybody into the AIM environment would be exceedingly bad policy. Eventually, through normal growth, IM services may become "mission critical" to companies; in that case they will likely install internal IM systems and might be reluctant to use free services anyway.[7]

Competing visions about what IM services should entail will generate constant threats of entry and ensure that optimal interoperability emerges—but in a market-driven, voluntary yet adversarial manner. Any improvements embraced by "interoperating" rivals could elevate them to a bargaining position sufficient to cut legitimate access deals with market leader AOL.

In a sense, we've been here before and things worked out fine. Lawrence Gasman has noted that, with respect to the broader telecommunications access debate, "Electronic mail networks pose equally complex interconnection problems. After all, three or four major national companies . . . and numerous smaller ones provide e-mail. It seems a daunting task to guarantee that an e-mail from one service provider could arrive in a competitor's box. The matter was left entirely to the private sector and has worked superbly."[8]

The idea that rivals should simply be handed access to a vast user/customer network they didn't help assemble and create, merely on the basis of declaring themselves to be in the instant messaging business, represents corporate regulatory pork and a vast overreach of government power. Under different circumstances, regulators would be arguing that everybody sharing a common network smacks of collusion and poses the threat of consumer exploitation.

PART III:

CONCLUSION

# 9. What Really Protects Consumers and Network Reliability—Markets or Mandates?

Advocates of forced access ignore the fact that innovation in devising networks is as important as other more typical types of market innovation exemplified in such mundane chores as devising products and services for consumers. Access regulation cannot mimic marketplace competition in keeping network technologies up to date and reliable. Under forced access, entrepreneurial incentives to undertake unique wiring projects, newfangled routing technologies, infrastructure maintenance, and, most importantly, *network replacement* are compromised because the evolution of the infrastructure remains too dependent on regulators.

Open access also creates an environment of continued pressures for reregulation, such as renewed calls for price caps on the regulated networks. Efficient, not administered, pricing and entry are necessary to guide capital, plan capacity, and locate new infrastructure. As Douglas Houston has noted with respect to electricity regulation, "A flaw in most transmission grid proposals is that they lack an explicit incentive for participants to alter capital without regulatory 'urging.'"[1] Regulated prices that are too low lead to skimping. Prices that are too high lead to "gold-plating" the network. It is highly unlikely that regulators will consistently hit the mark and generate efficient investment.

The ability to make and execute rational market strategies depends on whether the operator can exercise the owner's prerogative to exclude unwanted rivals, and thus whether he profits or loses from decisions. Mandatory access assures a prosperous future for regulators; under genuine competition, the regulator goes away.

Technological development and private control, rather than regulation, best protect the reliability of networks, a much-neglected fact that is especially relevant in the aftermath of the September 11, 2001, terrorist attacks, when the well-being of "critical infrastructure" has become a hot topic. Firms can be expected to offer various levels of reliability to meet customer needs. Any newcomer encroaching on incumbent territory seeking new business must make credible assurances of reliability. Reliability must be a competitive feature, not set at locked-in, regulated levels generated by the complacency that will inevitably accompany regulated access. Markets need to allow room for experimentation with both exclusionary and open-access models (both voluntary) to maximize reliability. To the extent that forced access biases the market toward a system in which many rather than few customers are affected by a given system failure, it is an impediment to, rather than a facilitator of, reliability. Policymakers should commit to nurturing a system whose shape will no longer depend on any regulatory authority making the right decisions. And that means avoiding open access or other central planning models.

Practicing regulatory restraint will allow policymakers to avoid tearing off scabs a few years from now to iron out the distortions created by mandatory access. No matter how many committee hearings, congressional workshops, or technical hearings on open access are held, and regardless of the supposed "independence" of overseers who promise "efficient" regulation and access, the desire of property owners to control their property will remain incompatible with the desires of opportunistic rivals who wish to hitch a ride uninvited. Instead, what is needed is the recognition of the vital role of private property rights in networks to prompt investment in viable, dynamic, reliable systems. For long-term success and innovation, competing (or, for that matter, cooperating) network owners must own the rights to future profits from innovation.

Everybody wins if policymakers avoid and abandon inefficient open-access regulatory regimes. Network owners win because they retain rights over their systems, can charge what the market will bear rather than a regulated price, need not surrender control of their network to a regulator, and can potentially invade the territory of rivals. Throughout and across many industries, business decisions would no longer be based on waiting for assorted jurisdictions to implement open access. Consumers win too, in that networks develop naturally and are more robust and reliable because newcomers must demonstrate competence and because innovations become necessary, competitive features rather than regulated ones.

While the "new" information economy is still new, it is an appropriate time to disabuse bureaucrats of the illusion that they are indispensable to competitive markets. Economists who accept as an article of faith the idea that capitalism generates "natural" monopolies apart from a government-granted franchise need to learn the same lesson. The mandates supported by both these groups are incompatible with the flourishing of networks. Now that the opportunity to ground the success of network industries firmly in property rights and contracts is at hand, strengthening regulatory intervention is the wrong thing to do.

# Notes

## Introduction

1. See, for example, Clyde Wayne Crews Jr., "Electric Avenues: Why 'Open Access' Can't Compete," Cato Institute Policy Analysis no. 301, April 13, 1998, http://www.cato.org/pubs/pas/pa-301es.html.

2. See William E. Lee, "Open Access, Private Interests, and the Emerging Broadband Market," Cato Institute Policy Analysis no. 379, August 29, 2000, http://www.cato.org/pubs/pas/pa-379es.html.

3. See John Ryan, "Infinite Loop: The Battle over Local Telecom Regulation," *The Ryan Perspective*, RHK Telecommunications Industry Analysts, March 2002; Yochi J. Dreazen, "AT&T Ratchets Up Efforts in Washington Pushing Bell Breakup Plan," *Wall Street Journal*, August 28, 2001, p. A16.

4. See Adam Thierer, "Structural Separation of the Bells—An Idea Whose Time Has Passed," Cato Institute *TechKnowledge* no. 17, August 20, 2001, http://www.cato.org/tech/tk/010820-tk.html; Wayne Crews and Adam Thierer, "The Digital Dirty Dozen: The Most Destructive High-Tech Legislation of the 107th Congress," Cato Institute Policy Analysis no. 423, February 4, 2002, pp. 5–6, http://www.cato.org/pubs/pas/pa-423es.html; and Adam Thierer, "Two Bizarre and Backward Ideas for Broadband Deployment," Cato Institute *TechKnowledge* no. 9, May 23, 2001, http://www.cato.org/tech/tk/010523-tk.html.

5. See Alan Reynolds, "The Microsoft Antitrust Appeal: Judge Jackson's 'Findings of Fact' Revisited" (Westfield, Ind.: Hudson Institute Publications, 2001).

## Chapter 1

1. For perhaps the most articulate expression of this pro–open access manifesto, see Jerry Berman, Alan Davidson, and Paula Bruening, "Comments of the Center for Democracy and Technology in the Matter of Inquiry Concerning High-Speed Access to the Internet over Cable and Other Facilities," Federal Communications Commission GN Docket No. 00-185, December 1, 2000, http://www.cdt.org/digi_infra/broadband/001201fcc.shtml.

2. James K. Glassman, "The FCC's Dangerous Internet Precedent," *Wall Street Journal*, January 17, 2001, p. A26.

3. J. Gregory Sidak and Daniel F. Spulber, *Deregulatory Takings and the Regulatory Contract: The Competitive Transformation of Network Industries in the United States* (Cambridge, England: Cambridge University Press, 1997).

4. J. Gregory Sidak and Daniel F. Spulber, "Givings, Takings, and the Fallacy of Forward-Looking Costs," *New York University Law Review* 72, no. 5 (1997): 1076.

5. Adam D. Thierer, "Separating Fact from Fiction in the Debate over Stranded Cost Recovery," Heritage Foundation Talking Points no. 20, March 11, 1997.

6. Laurence H. Tribe, "Why the Commission Should Not Adopt a Broad View of the 'Primary Video' Carriage Obligation," Ex Parte filing of the National Cable Television Association, *In the Matter of Carriage of Digital Television Broadcast Signals*, CS Docket 98-120, July 9, 2002, p. 12 [emphasis in original], http://www.ncta.com/pdf_files/ExParte_Tribe.doc.pdf.

7. Roger Pilon, "A Modest Proposal on 'Must-Carry,' the 1992 Cable Act, and Regulation Generally: Go Back to Basics," *Hastings Communications and Entertainment Law Journal* 17, no. 1 (Fall 1994): 59.

8. *Bell Atlantic Corp. v. FCC*, 24 F. 3d, 1441, D.C. Circuit, 1994.

9. *Loretto v. Teleprompter Manhattan CATV Corp.*, 458 U.S. 419, 1982.

10. David Kopel, "Comments of the Heartland Institute," *In the Matter of Inquiry Concerning High-Speed Access to Internet over Cable and Other Facilities*, GEN Docket No. 00-185, December 1, 2000, p. 59.

11. Daniel F. Spulber and Christopher S. Yoo, "Access to Networks: Economic and Constitutional Connections," *Cornell Law Review* (May 2003) (forthcoming): 11.

12. C. Michael Armstrong, "Telecom and Cable TV: Shared Prospects for the Communications Future," Address to the Washington Metropolitan Cable Club, Washington, D.C., November 2, 1998.

13. John C. Wohlstetter, "The Vulnerability of Networks," *Regulation* 24, no. 4 (Winter 2001): 50.

14. Alfred E. Kahn, "Declaration of Alfred E. Kahn in Response to Second Further Notice of Proposed Rulemaking," *In the Matter of Implementation of the Local Competition Provisions in the Telecommunications Act of 1996*, Federal Communications Commission CC Docket No. 96-98, 1998 p. 17.

15. Justice Stephen Breyer, *AT&T Corporation et al. v. Iowa Utilities Board*, January 25, 1999.

16. See William E. Lee, "Open Access, Private Interests, and the Emerging Broadband Market," Cato Institute Policy Analysis no. 379, August 29, 2000, http://www.cato.org/pubs/pas/pa379.pdf.

17. "Net Gains and Losses," *Wall Street Journal*, December 18, 2000, p. A22.

18. Elizabeth Wasserman, "The Other Side of the Aisle: From Disney to EarthLink to Bell South, an All-Star List of Enemies Has Come Together to Fight the Merger of AOL and Time Warner," *The Industry Standard*, October 30, 2000, p. 171.

19. P. H. Longstaff, *The Communications Toolkit: How to Build and Regulate Any Communications Business* (Cambridge, Mass.: MIT Press, 2002), p. 71.

20. See generally Peter Van Doren, "Making Sense of Electricity Deregulation," *Regulation* 23, no. 3 (Summer 2000): 68–72, http://www.cato.org/pubs/regulation/regv23n3/vandoren.pdf.

21. Christopher Wolf, "Letter to the Editor," *Wall Street Journal*, July 28, 1999, p. A23.

22. Lawrence Gasman, "Access in Telecommunications," *Regulation* 20, no. 2 (Spring 1997): 40.

23. Robert Crandall, "Managed Competition in U.S. Telecommunications," AEI-Brookings Joint Center for Regulatory Studies Working Paper 99-1, March 1999, p. 13, http://www.aei.brookings.org/publications/working/working_99_01.pdf

24. *Verizon Communications Inc. v. Federal Communications Commission*, 535 U.S. ___ (2002), http://a257.g.akamaitech.net/7/257/2422/29apr20021100/www.supremecourtus.gov/opinions/01pdf/00-511.pdf

25. See Dick Kelsey, "Supreme Court Rules FCC Can Set Pole Rates," *Newsbytes*, January 16, 2002, http://www.newsbytes.com/news/02/173700.html.

26. Cited in Kelsey.

27. Noted in Kelsey and also in Joan Biscupic, "Justices Hear Cable-Internet Fee Dispute," *USA Today*, October 2, 2001, http://www.usatoday.com/news/court/2001-10-03-cable-fee.htm.

28. It is worth noting that the current FCC commissioner, Michael Powell, is taking steps to reverse much of this agenda by scaling back many of the burdensome infrastructure-sharing mandates imposed by the agency before his tenure. See Adam Thierer, "How Four FCC Rulemakings Could Finally Break the Broadband Logjam," Cato Institute *TechKnowledge* no. 34, March 28, 2002, http://www.cato.org/tech/tk/020328-tk.html.

29. Adam D. Thierer, "Broadband Telecommunications for the 21st Century: Five Principles for Reform," Heritage Foundation Backgrounder no. 1317, September 1, 1999, p. 23, http://www.heritage.org/library/backgrounder/bg1317.html.

30. J. Gregory Sidak, "The Failure of Good Intentions: The Collapse of American Telecommunications after Six Years of Deregulation," *2002 Beesley Lecture on Regulation*, The Royal Society of Arts, October 1, 2002, http://papers.ssrn.com/sol3/delivery.cfm/SSRN_ID335180_code021001500.pdf?abstractid = 335180.

31. Adam Thierer and Lucas Mast, "Digital Divide Update: The Rhetoric Finally Matches the Reality," Cato Institute *TechKnowledge* no. 33, February 27, 2002, http://www.cato.org/tech/tk/020227-tk.html.

32. *Colorado Revised Statutes*, Title 40 (Utilities), Article 5, New Construction—Extension, Section 40-5-101.

33. See *Turner Broadcasting System, Inc. v. FCC*, 512 U.S. 622 (1994), and *Turner Broadcasting System, Inc v. FCC*, 520 U.S. 180 (1997).

## Chapter 2

1. Richard A. Posner, *Natural Monopoly and Its Regulation*, 30th Anniversary Edition (Washington: Cato Institute, 1999), p. v.

2. W. Kip Viscusi, John M. Vernon, and Joseph E. Harrington, *Economics of Regulation and Antitrust*, 2d ed. (Cambridge, Mass.: MIT Press, 1998), p. 351.

3. Glen O. Robinson, "On Refusing to Deal with Rivals," UVA Law and Economics Research Paper no. 01-3 (Abstract), May 2001, http://papers.ssrn.com/sol3/papers.cfm?abstract_id = 269130.

4. Dominick T. Armentano, *Antitrust and Monopoly: Anatomy of a Policy Failure* (New York: Holmes & Meier, 1982), p. 3.

5. James R. Nelson, "The Role of Competition in the Regulated Industries," *Antitrust Bulletin* XI (January–April 1966): 3.

6. Thomas Hazlett, "The Curious Evolution of Natural Monopoly Theory," in *Unnatural Monopolies: The Case for Deregulating Public Utilities*, ed. Robert W. Poole (Lexington, Mass.: Lexington Books, 1985), p. 21.

7. Phillip Areeda, "Essential Facilities: An Epithet in Need of Limiting Principles," *Antitrust Law Journal* (1990): 841.

8. *Flip Side Prods., Inc. v. Jam Prods., Ltd.*, 843 F. 2d 1024 (7th Circuit), cert denied, 109 S. Ct. 261 (1988).

9. *Olympia Equip. Leasing Co. v. Western Union Tel. Co.*, 797 F. 2d 370 (7th Circuit, 1986), cert. denied, 107 S. Ct. 1574 (1987).

10. *Aspen Ski Co. v. Aspen Highlands Skiing Corp.*, 472 U.S. 585 (1985).

11. *Twin Laboratories, Inc. v. Weider Health & Fitness Corp.*, 720 F. Supp. 31 (S.D.N.Y., 1989).

12. *Northwest Wholesale Stationers, Inc. v. Pacific Stationery & Printing Co.*, 472 U.S. 284 (1985).

13. *Jefferson Parish Hosp. Dist. No. 2 v. Hyde*, 466 U.S. 2 (1984).

14. *Florida Fuels, Inc. v. Belcher Oil Co.*, 717 F. Supp. 1528 (S.D. Fla., 1989).

15. *Berkey Photo v. Eastman Kodak Co.*, 603 F. 2d 263 (2d Circuit, 1979), cert. denied, 444 U.S. 1063 (1980).

16. Abbott B. Lipsky Jr. and J. Gregory Sidak, "Essential Facilities," *Stanford Law Review* 51 (May 1999): 1187.

17. Lawrence J. White, *U.S. Public Policy toward Network Industries* (Washington: AEI-Brookings Joint Center for Regulatory Studies, 1999), pp. 27–28.

18. James R. Ratner, "Should There Be an Essential Facilities Doctrine?" *University of California Davis Law Review* (Winter 1998): 328.

19. Longstaff.

20. Gerald W. Brock, *The Telecommunications Industry: The Dynamics of Market Structure* (Cambridge, Mass.: Harvard University Press, 1981), p. 112.

21. Ibid., p. 111.

22. Leonard S. Hyman, Richard C. Toole, and Rosemary M. Avellis, *The New Telecommunications Industry: Evolution and Organization* 1 (Vienna, Va.: Public Utility Reports, Inc., 1987), p. 78.

23. Brock, p. 122.

24. Hyman et al., p. 90.

25. For extensive details, see Adam D. Thierer, "Unnatural Monopoly: Critical Moments in the Development of the Bell System Monopoly," *Cato Journal* 14, no. 2 (Fall 1994): 267–85, http://www.cato.org/pubs/journal/cjv14n2-6.html.

26. Brock, p. 156.

27. Peter W. Huber, Michael K. Kellogg, and John Thorne, *Federal Telecommunications Law* (New York: Aspen Law & Business, 1999), p. 17.

28. F. A. Hayek, "The Meaning of Competition," in *Individualism and the Economic Order* (Chicago: University of Chicago Press, 1948).

29. Israel M. Kirzner, *Competition and Entrepreneurship* (Chicago: University of Chicago Press, 1973); and Israel M. Kirzner, *Discovery and the Capitalist Process* (Chicago: University of Chicago Press, 1985).

30. Thomas Hazlett, "The Curious Evolution of Natural Monopoly Theory," in *Unnatural Monopolies: The Case for Deregulating Public Utilities*, ed. Robert W. Poole (Lexington, Mass.: Lexington Books, 1985), p. 18.

31. Milton Friedman, *Capitalism and Freedom* (Chicago: University of Chicago Press, 1962), p. 128.

32. Posner, p. 7.

33. Ibid., p. 14.

34. Viscusi et al., p. 513.

35. George Stigler, "The Theory of Economic Regulation," *Bell Journal of Economics and Management Science* 2, no. 1 (Spring 1971), reprinted in *The Essence of Stigler*, ed. Kurt R. Leube and Thomas Gale Moore (Stanford, Calif.: Hoover Institution Press, 1986), p. 243.

36. In particular, see Sam Peltzman, "Toward a More General Theory of Regulation," *Journal of Law and Economics* 19 (August 1976): 211–40.

37. For a broader discussion of Stigler's theory of regulation and a comparison to other modern theories of regulation, see David L. Kaserman and John W. Mayo, *Government and Business: The Economics of Antitrust and Regulation* (Fort Worth, Tex.: Dryden Press, 1995), pp. 517–44.

38. Milton Friedman, *Capitalism and Freedom* (Chicago: University of Chicago Press, 1962), pp. 128–29.

39. Alfred E. Kahn, *The Economics of Regulation: Principles and Institutions* 2 (Cambridge, Mass.: MIT Press, 1988), p. 12. Kahn elaborates on the dangers of a cozy regulator-regulatee relationship: "Responsible for the continued provision and improvement of service, [the regulatory commission] comes increasingly and understandably to identify the interest of the public with that of the existing companies on whom it must rely to deliver goods." Ibid., p. 46.

40. Posner, p. 92.

41. Richard H. K. Vietor, *Contrived Competition: Regulation and Deregulation in America* (Cambridge, Mass.: Harvard University Press, 1994), p. 315.

42. White, p. 14.

## Chapter 3

1. Steve G. Steinberg, "Telecom Goes Qwest," *Wired*, March 1998, p. 91.

2. Ibid., p. 91.

3. Rachel King, "Too Much Long Distance," *Fortune*, March 19, 1999, p. 107, http://www.business2.com/articles/mag/0,1640,4516,FF.html.

4. In a letter to the editor of the *Wall Street Journal*, Level 3 president and CEO James Crowe noted, "We have consistently told the Justice Department, the European Commission, the FCC and anyone else who will listen that competition in communications, like other 'networked' industries such as electric power, railroads and airlines, depends on open, cost-effective and nondiscriminatory interconnection of the networks of competing companies," and that mergers should be conditioned on "principles of open and fair interconnection," July 14, 2000. p. A15.

5. See http://www.globalstar.com/partner_information.html.

6. See http://www.teledesic.com/partners/partners.htm.

7. Mike Mills, "Undersea Cables Carry Growing Rivers of Data," *Washington Post*, March 9, 1998, p. A01, http://www.washingtonpost.com/wp-srv/national/longterm/oceans/stories/cables030998.htm.

8. See, for example, Peter S. Goodman, "Linking Old Economy to New: Many Utilities Are Finding the Telecom Industry a Natural Extension," *Washington Post*, June 6, 2000, p. E1.

9. Nancy Gohring, "Wireless Giants Go for Sharing," *Interactive Week*, June 18, 2001, http://www.zdnet.com/filters/printerfriendly/0,6061,2775971-35,00.html.

10. Ben Charny, "High Costs Push Wireless Carriers to Share," *CNET News.com*, October 15, 2001, http://news. com.com/2100-1033-274417.html?legacy=cnet.

11. Stephen C. Fehr, "D.C.'s High-Tech Highways Wreaking Havoc on Traffic," *Washington Post*, March 21, 1999, p. A19.

12. Stephen C. Fehr, "The Work below the Streets," *Washington Post*, March 21, 1999, p. A19.

13. Steve Gelsi, "CityNet Using Wet Last Mile," *CBS.MarketWatch.com*, August 16, 2001. See also Yuki Noguchi, "CityNet Wins $275 Million in Funding," *Washington Post*, April 10, 2001, p. E5, http://www.washtech.com/ news/telecom/8919-1.html.

14. Evan Ramstad and Kortney Stringer, "In Race to Lay Fiber, Telecoms Wreak Havoc on City Streets," *Wall Street Journal*, February 27, 2001, p. A1.

15. See Jacques R. Bughin, Renee C. Foster, Alan Miles, and Luis A. Ubiñas, "Home Is Where the Network Is," *McKinsey Quarterly*, no. 2, 2001, http://www.mckinsey quarterly.com/article_page.asp?ar = 1010&L2 = 38&L3 = 100&srid = 12&gp = 1

16. Dan Caterinicchia, "Many New Houston Homes Will Be Internet-Wired," *CNN*, July 13, 1999, http://www.cnn.com/TECH/computing/9907/13/housewired.idg/.

17. Noted in Robin Lloyd, "Houston Firm Wires the 'Last Mile,'" *CNN Interactive*, August 6, 1999, http://www.cnn.com/TECH/ptech/9908/06/wiring.ptech/.

18. Mike Mills, "For the Plugged-In Buyer, a House That Jacks Built," *Washington Post*, January 21, 1998, p. E1.

19. See "Fetish," *Wired*, August 1997, http://www.wired.com/wired/archive/5.08/fetish.html.

20. Ibid.

21. Richard A. Oppel Jr., "Internet-Ready Houses Are Finding a Home," *New York Times*, May 26, 2001, p. A1.

22. Ibid.

23. Ibid.

## Chapter 4

1. Michael Powell, "Local Competition . . . CLECs in the Midst of an Explosion," Speech before the Association of Local Telecommunications Services, December 2, 1998, http://www.fcc.gov/Speeches/Powell/spmkp819.txt.

2. For a comprehensive overview of the electric power industry and the state of deregulation, see Peter Van Doren, "The Deregulation of the Electricity Industry: A Primer," Cato Institute Policy Analysis no. 320, October 6, 1998, http://www.cato.org/pubs/pas/pa-320.pdf.

3. Edward Walsh, "High Court Upholds Power Line Opening," *Washington Post*, March 5, 2002, p. A8.

4. See Jerry Taylor, "Enron Was No Friend to Free Markets," *Wall Street Journal*, January 21, 2002, http://www.cato.org/research/articles/taylor-020121.html.

5. Noted in Walsh.

6. On the California electricity crisis, see Jerry Taylor and Peter Van Doren, "California's Electricity Crisis: What's Going On, Who's to Blame, and What to Do," Cato Institute Policy Analysis no. 406, http://www.cato.org/pubs/pas/pa-406es.html.

7. See Robert Michaels, "Stranded Investments, Stranded Intellectuals," *Regulation* 19, no. 1 (Winter 1996), http://www.cato.org/pubs/regulation/reg19n1b.html

8. See, for example, "FERC Judge Issues Blueprint for Northeast RTO," *Energy User News*, November 5, 2001, http://www.energyusernews.com/CDA/Article Information/features/BNP_Features_Item/0,2584,67023,00.html.

9. See Richard E. Balzhiser, "Technology: It's Only Begun to Make a Difference," *Electricity Journal* (May 1996).

10. Stuart F. Brown, "Here Come the Pint-Size Power Plants," *Fortune*, April 1, 1996, p. 64D.

11. George T. Preston and Dan Rastler, "Distributed Generation: Competitive Threat or Opportunity," *Public Utilities Fortnightly*, August 1996, p. 13.

12. "Big Future for Distributed Generation," *Electricity Daily*, Sept. 30, 1998, p. 1.

13. Ibid.

14. Margaret Kriz, "Power Brokers," *National Journal*, November 30, 1996, p. 2596.

15. Richard E. Balzhiser, "Technology to Play Hand in Future Power Market," *Forum for Applied Research and Public Policy*, Fall 1997, p. 25.

16. Ibid.

17. Robert Bryce, "Division of Power: Powerline Access Surges Abroad, Shorts Out in U.S.," *Interactive Week*, April 23, 2001, pp. 39–42.

18. Ibid.

19. "Loopy," *The Economist*, September 9, 2000, pp. 100–101.

20. For an important overview, see Douglas A. Houston, "User-Ownership of Electric Transmission Grids: Toward Resolving the Access Issue," *Regulation*, Winter 1992, pp. 48–57.

## Chapter 5

1. Telecommunications Act of 1996, Public Law No. 106-106, 47 U.S.C. §151, February 8, 1996.

2. Federal Communications Commission, "Implementation of the Local Competition Provisions of the Telecommunications Act of 1996," First Report and Order, FCC Docket No. 96-325, August 8, 1996, http://www.fcc.gov/Bureaus/Common_Carrier/Orders/1996/fcc96325.pdf.

3. List taken from Huber et al., pp. 507–522.

4. *AT&T v. Iowa Utilities Board*, 525 U.S. 366 (1999), http://caselaw.lp.findlaw.com/cgi-bin/getcase.pl?court = US&navby = case&vol = 000&invol = 97-826.

5. As Eli Noam, professor of economics and finance at the Columbia Business School, summarized in a recent editorial, "When in 1996 the Telecom was passed, many people hailed it as a Magna Carta of deregulation. It is turning out to be the enabler of long-term regulatory intervention and of a centralization of regulation in Washington. Ironically, it is the economic conservatives on the Supreme Court who have now sanctioned this expansion of central regulatory powers." See Eli Noam, "Regulating in Order to Deregulate," *FT.com*, May 22, 2002.

6. For example, see Federal Communications Commission, "Deployment of Wireline Services Offering Advanced Telecommunications Capability," CC Docket Nos. 98-147, et al., FCC 98-188, August 7, 1998, http://www.fcc.gov/Bureaus/Common_Carrier/News_Releases/1998/nrcc8057.html.

7. Robert Crandall, "Managed Competition in U.S. Telecommunications," AEI-Brookings Joint Center for Regulatory Studies Working Paper 99-1, March 1999, p. 12, http://www.aei.brookings.org/publications/working/working_99_01.pdf.

8. Noam.

9. Ibid.

10. Alfred E. Kahn, "Resisting the Temptation to Micromanage: Lessons from Airlines and Trucking," in *Regulators' Revenge: The Future of Telecommunications Deregulation*, ed. Tom W. Bell and Solveig Singleton (Washington: Cato Institute, 1998), p. 27.

11. George Gilder, *Telecosm: How Infinite Bandwidth Will Revolutionize Our World* (New York: Free Press, 2000).

12. George Gilder, "Tumbling into the Telechasm," *Wall Street Journal*, August 6, 2001, p. A12.

13. Ibid.

14. J. Gregory Sidak, Hal J. Singer, and David J. Teece, "A General Framework for Competitive Analysis in Wireless Telecommunications," *Hastings Law Journal* 50 (1999): 1639.

15. Ibid.

16. Federal Communications Commission, *Annual Report and Analysis of Competitive Market Conditions with Respect to Commercial Mobile Services*, Seventh Report, FCC 02-179, July 3, 2002, p. 32, http://hraunfoss.fcc.gov/edocs_public/attachmatch/FCC-02-179A2.pdf.

17. Michelle Kessler, "18% See Cell Phones as Their Main Phones," *USA Today*, January 31, 2002, http://www.usatoday.com/money/tech/2002-02-01-cell-phones.htm.

18. Ibid.

19. "20 Million Access Lines Lost to Wireless, Study Says," *MobileInfo.com*, Issue no. 2002-03, January 2002, http://www.mobileinfo.com/News_2002/Issue03/IDC_study.htm

20. "New Study Reveals Mobile Carrier Threat to Wireline," Cellular Telecommunications and Internet Association, *Wireless Newsline Releases*, June 3, 2002, http://www.wow-com.com/news/wireless_newslines/press_release.cfm?press_id=4083.

21. Scott Woolley, "Bad Connection," *Forbes.com*, August 12, 2002, http://www.forbes.com/forbes/2002/0812/084.html.

22. See http://www.wow-com.com/.

23. See "Industry Issues and Answers: Competition, Innovation, and Safety," Cellular Telecommunications and Internet Association, http://www.wow-com.com/industry/policy/cong_affairs/articles.cfm?ID=366.

24. Robert W. Crandall and Jerry A. Hausman, "Competition in U.S. Telecommunications Services: Effects of the 1996 Legislation," in *Deregulation of Network Industries: What's Next?* ed. Sam Peltzman and Clifford Winston (Washington: AEI-Brookings Joint Center for Regulatory Studies, 2000), p. 86.

25. John Thorne, *The 1996 Telecom Act: What Went Wrong and Protecting the Broadband Buildout* (Washington: Verizon Communications, 2001), p. 6.

26. Ibid.

27. See Adam Thierer, "Forced Access Follies Continue: The Case of Special Access Services," Cato Institute *TechKnowledge* no. 32, January 28, 2002, http://www.cato.org/tech/tk/020128-tk.html.

28. See Katie Hafner, "Group Is Said to Accuse Pacific Bell of Monopoly," *New York Times*, July 26, 2001, http://college3.nytimes.com/guests/articles/2001/07/26/858919.xml.

29. Justice Stephen Breyer, *AT&T Corp. v. Iowa Utilities Board*, 529 U.S. 429, 1999 (emphasis in original).

30. Robert Crandall, *An Assessment of the Competitive Local Exchange Carriers Five Years after the Passage of the Telecommunications Act*, Criterion Economics, L.L.C., June 2001, p. 4 (emphasis in original).

31. Ibid., p. 5.

32. Also see Larry F. Darby, Jeffrey A. Eisenach, and Joseph S. Kraemer, "The CLEC Experiment: Anatomy of a Meltdown," Progress and Freedom Foundation, *Progress on Point*, Release 9.23, September 2002.

33. Seth Schiesel, "Seizing the Phone Giants' Turf; Upstart RCN Digs in Despite Industry's Turmoil," *New York Times*, April 9, 2001, p. C1.

34. Thomas M. Jorde, J. Gregory Sidak, and David J. Teece, "Innovation, Investment, and Unbundling," *Yale Journal of Regulation* 17, no. 1 (2000): 8.

35. Scott C. Cleland, *Why De-Regulation Is Now the Dominant Telecom Trend/Theme* (Washington: The Precursor Group, November 28, 2001) (emphasis in original).

36. Peter Huber, "Washington Created WorldCom," *Wall Street Journal*, July 1, 2002, p. A14.

37. Ibid.

38. See Adam Thierer, "Structural Separation of the Bells—An Idea Whose Time Has Passed," Cato Institute *TechKnowledge* no. 17, August 20, 2001, http://www.cato.org/tech/tk/010820-tk.html; Wayne Crews and Adam Thierer, "The Digital Dirty Dozen: The Most Destructive High-Tech Legislation of the 107th Congress," Cato Institute Policy Analysis no. 423, February 4, 2002, pp. 5–6, http://www.cato.org/pubs/pas/pa-423es.html; and Robert Crandall and J. Gregory Sidak, "Is Structural Separation of Incumbent Local Exchange Carriers Necessary for Competition?" *Yale Journal of Regulation* 19, no. 2 (2002).

39. Huber et al., p. 957.

## Chapter 6

1. Quoted in Corey Grice, "The Next Wave in Fast Net Access," *CNET News.com*, July 28, 1999, http://news.com.com/2009-1033-227295.html?legacy=cnet.

2. OpenNet Coalition, "What's at Stake: High Speed Access," http://www.opennetcoalition.org/what/index.html.

3. Quoted in Jeff Chester and Gary O. Larson, "End of the Open Road?" *The American Prospect* 11, no. 5 (January 17, 2000), http://www.prospect.org/print/V11/5/chester-j.html.

4. Noted in M. J. Zuckerman, " 'Race Is Fierce' to Broadband Sales," *USA Today*, June 26, 2000, http://www.usatoday.com/life/cyber/bonus/0600/cb012.htm.

5. Noted in Stephen Manes, "Dispelling Those Bandwidth Myths," *CNN*, February 8, 1999, http://www.cnn.com/TECH/computing/9902/08/bandmyth.idg/index. html. See also Tim Greene, "DSL Has a Secret," *CNN.com*, March 2, 1999, http://www.cnn.com/TECH/computing/9903/02/dslsecret.idg/.

6. Federal Communications Commission, "Third Report Concerning the Deployment of Advanced Telecommunications Capability," CC Docket 98-146, February 6, 2002, http://www.fcc.gov/Bureaus/Common_Carrier/News_Releases/2002/nrcc0201.html

7. Antonio A. Prado, "Are Antitrust Laws Obsolete in the New Economy?" *Investor's Business Daily*, April 16, 2001, p. A6.

8. Lawrence Lessig, *Code and Other Laws of Cyberspace* (New York: Basic Books, 1999).

9. Lawrence Lessig, "Straitjacket on the Internet?" *Washington Post*, October 25, 2000, p. A31.

10. In 1999, AT&T purchased Tele-Communications Inc., the second largest cable-TV operator for $55 billion, and then later acquired MediaOne, the third largest cable provider, for $58 billion.

11. Kara Swisher, Khanh Tran, and Kathy Chen, "High-Stakes Internet Battle Erupts in San Francisco," *Wall Street Journal*, July 26, 1999, p. A24; and Joyce E. Cutler, "San Francisco Agency Urges Access to Net on Cable Broadband by 2003," *BNA Daily Report for Executives*, January 21, 2000, p. A-23.

12. "Florida County Follows Portland Move to Hit Cable Data Effort with Open Access," *BNA Daily Report for Executives*, July 15, 1999, p. A-45.

13. David Kaut, "Miami-Dade Council Refuses to Impose Internet-Access Duties on Broadband Cable," *BNA Daily Report for Executives*, October 20, 1999, p. A-32.

14. Kip Betz, "Boosting Trend, St. Louis Seen Poised to Require Cable to Open Internet Access," *BNA Daily Report for Executives*, October 27, 1999, p. A-36.

15. David Kaut, "Cambridge Joins List of Communities Requiring Cable Internet-Access Duties," *BNA Daily Report for Executives*, October 25, 1999, p. A-15.

16. Peter Elstrom, Ronald Grover, and Catherine Yang, "Whose Cables Are They?" *Business Week*, July 5, 1999, pp. 24–26.

17. C. Michael Armstrong, "Telecom and Cable TV: Shared Prospects for the Communications Future," Address to the Washington Metropolitan Cable Club, Washington, D.C., November 2, 1998.

18. *AT&T Corp. v. City of Portland*, Ninth Circuit Court of Appeals, D.C. No. CV-99-00065-OMP, June 22, 2000.

19. John Schwartz, AT&T Wins Internet Decision," *Washington Post*, June 23, 2000, p. E1; and Julia Angwin and Jill Carroll, "Judge Rules for AT&T in Cable-Access Dispute," *Wall Street Journal*, June 23, 2000, p. A3.

20. Matt Richtel, "Both Sides Talk of Victory in Cable Ruling," *New York Times*, June 23, 2000, p. C2.

21. Jim Davis and Corey Grice, "FCC's Kennard Slams Open Access Ruling," *CNET News.com*, June 15, 1999, http://news.com.com/2100-1033-227121.html?tag = rn.

22. William E. Kennard, "How to End the World Wide Wait," *Wall Street Journal*, August 24, 1999, p. A18.

23. Kathy Chen, "FCC Chairman Calls for National Policy on High-Speed Internet Access Via Cable," *Wall Street Journal*, July 16, 1999, p. B4.

24. William E. Kennard, "Remarks before the National Cable Television Association," June 15, 1999, http://www.fcc.gov/Speeches/Kennard/spwek921.html.

25. Ibid.

26. "In the Matter of Inquiry Concerning High-Speed Access to the Internet Over Cable and Other Facilities," Federal Communications Commission, GN Docket No. 00-185, September 28, 2000, http://www.fcc.gov/Bureaus/ Miscellaneous/Notices/ 2000/fcc00355.pdf

27. Adam Thierer, "How Four FCC Proceedings Could Finally Break the Broadband Logjam," Cato Institute *TechKnowledge* no. 34, March 28, 2002, http://www. cato.org/tech/tk/020328-tk.html.

28. Brigitte Greenberg, "Ninth Circuit Will Hear Landmark Case on Cable Modem Service," *Washington Internet Daily* 3, No. 63, p. 1.

29. Lessig, "Straitjacket on the Internet?"; and Mark A. Lemley and Lawrence Lessig, "The End of End-to-End: Preserving the Architecture of the Internet in the Broadband Era," Stanford University School of Law Working Paper no. 207, 2000.

30. Christopher Stern, "FCC Gives Cable Firms Net Rights," *Washington Post*, March 15, 2002, p. E1.

31. Robert MacMillan, "Cable ISPs Not Required to Share Network—FCC," *Newsbytes*, March 14, 2002, http://www.newsbytes.com/news/02/175217.html.

32. "I am persuaded that open access to *all* transmission media is the only way to guarantee that every ISP can reach every possible subscriber by every means available." Quoted in Patrick Ross, "Cerf Urges FCC and Commerce to Embrace Open Broadband Networks," *Washington Internet Daily*, May 21, 2002, pp. 3–4.

33. Vinton G. Cerf, "Don't Give AT&T a New Monopoly," *Wall Street Journal*, July 27, 1999, p. A22.

34. John Borland, "Sprint, WorldCom Call Off $120 Billion Merger," *CNET News.com*, July 13, 2000, http://news.com.com/2100-1033-243110.html?legacy = cnet.

35. George Gilder, "Open Access Now! Wait, Never Mind," *Wall Street Journal*, February 18, 2000, p. A14.

36. See, for example, *Transforming the Information Superhighway into a Private Toll Road: The Case against Closed Access Broadband Internet Systems*, Consumer Federation of America, September 1999, http://www.massopenaccess.org/pdf/cfasep99.pdf.

37. http://www.opennetcoalition.org/.

38. Wasserman, p. 171.

39. "Net Gains and Losses," *Wall Street Journal*, December 18, 2000, p. A22.

40. "MindSpring Wants Cable Access," *Reuters*, April 14, 1999.

41. Jube Shiver, "Broadband Firms Can Close Their Networks," *Los Angeles Times*, March 15, 2002, http://www.latimes.com/technology/la-000018923mar15.story.

42. Ibid.

43. Holman W. Jenkins Jr., "How a Telecom Meltdown Will Cause the Next Recession," *Wall Street Journal*, September 27, 2000, p. A27.

44. Holman W. Jenkins Jr., "Let's Have a Closed Access Free-for-All," *Wall Street Journal*, January 26, 2000, p. A23.

45. Douglas S. Shapiro, "Uncommon Carriers," *Decoding the Signals*, Deutsche Bank Securities, October 19, 1998, pp. 3–4.

46. Michael Powell, *Remarks at the National Summit on Broadband Deployment*, October 25, 2001, p. 18.

47. Lawrence J. White, *U.S. Public Policy toward Network Industries* (Washington: AEI-Brookings Joint Center for Regulatory Studies, 1999), p. 20.

48. Steve Steinberg, "Hype List," *Wired*, September 1997, p. 80, http://www.wired.com/wired/archive/5.09/hypelist_pr.html.

49. David B. Kopel, "Access to the Internet: Regulation or Markets?" Heartland Institute, Heartland Policy Study no. 92, September 24, 1999, p. 3, http://www.heartland.org/studies/kopel-sum.htm.

50. David B. Kopel, "Comments of the Heartland Institute," *In the Matter of Inquiry Concerning High-Speed Access to Internet over Cable and Other Facilities*, GEN Docket No. 00-185, December 1, 2000, p. 59.

51. Thomas W. Hazlett and George Bittlingmayer, "The Political Economy of Cable 'Open Access,'" AEI-Brookings Joint Center for Regulatory Studies Working Paper no. 01-06, May 2001, p. 57, http://www.aei.brookings.org/publications/working/working_01_06.pdf.

52. "Boucher Says He's Drafting a Revised Open Access Bill," *Washington Internet Daily*, July 13, 2001, p. 1. The congressman reiterated this intention in February 2002. Robert MacMillan, "Rep. Boucher Plans Privacy, Open Access Bills," *Newsbytes*, February 13, 2002, http://www.newsbytes.com/news/02/174484.html.

53. David McGuire, "Groups Vow Renewed Cable ISP Open-Access Fight," *Washington Post.com*, July 10, 2002, http://www.washingtonpost.com/wp-dyn/articles/A50363-2002Jul10.html.

54. Terry Lane, "ACLU Joins Consumer Groups on Cable Open Access Requirements," *Washington Internet Daily*, July 11, 2002, pp. 4–5.

55. Robert Crandall, "Competition Is the Key to Open Access," *Wall Street Journal*, December 13, 2000, p. 26.

56. Federal Communications Commission, *Implementation of the Local Competition Provisions of the Telecommunications Act of 1996*, First Report and Order, FCC Docket No. 96-325, August 8, 1996, http://www.fcc.gov/Bureaus/Common_Carrier/Orders/1996/fcc96325.pdf.

57. Federal Communications Commission, *Deployment of Wireline Services Offering Advanced Telecommunications Capability*, FCC Docket No. 98-188, August 7, 1998, http://www.fcc.gov/Bureaus/Common_Carrier/ News_Releases/1998/nrcc8057.html.

58. Federal Communications Commission, *In the Matter of Deployment of Wireline Services Offering Advanced Telecommunications Capability*, CC Docket No. 98-147, August 7, 1998, http://www.fcc.gov/Bureaus/Common_Carrier/Orders/1998/fcc98188.pdf.

59. Ibid.

60. Longstaff, p. 2.

61. Huber et al., p. 1072.

62. Ibid.

63. Federal Communications Commission, *In the Matter of Review of Section 251* "Unbundling Obligations Of Incumbent Local Exchange Carriers," CC Docket No. 01-338, December 12, 2001, http://hraunfoss.fcc.gov/edocs_public/attachmatch/FCC-01-361A1.pdf.

64. "In the Matter of Review of Regulatory Requirements for Incumbent LEC Broadband Telecommunications Services," Federal Communications Commission, CC Docket No. 01-337, December 12, 2001, http://hraunfoss.fcc.gov/edocs_public/attachmatch/FCC-01-360A1.pdf.

65. Federal Communications Commission, "In the Matter of Appropriate Framework for Broadband Access to the Internet over Wireline Facilities," CC Docket No. 02-33, February 14, 2002, http://hraunfoss.fcc.gov/edocs_public/ attachmatch/FCC-02-42A1.pdf.

66. Federal Communications Commission, "In the Matter of Inquiry Concerning High-Speed Access to the Internet over Cable and Other Facilities," GN Docket No. 00-185, September 28, 2000, http://www.fcc.gov/Bureaus/ Miscellaneous/Notices/2000/fcc00355.pdf.

67. Patrick Ross, "Most Commenters Urge FCC to Apply Unbundling to Bell DSL," *Washington Internet Daily*, July 3, 2002, pp. 2–5.

68. Randolph J. May, "Broadband Gets a Breaux-Nickles Boost," Progress and Freedom Foundation, *Progress on Point* 9.15, May 2002, http://www.pff.org/Publications/POP9.15BreauxNickles.pdf.

69. S. 2430, The Broadband Regulatory Parity Act of 2002, 107th Congress.

70. See Reinhart Krause, "Bells Will Battle for Their Fiber, Dominant Carriers Struggle with Regulators over How They Must Share Networks," *Investor's Business Daily*, June 15, 2002, p. A16.

71. Noted in Craig Kuhl, "Fiber-to-the-Home Deployment Inches Forward," *Communications Engineering & Design*, October 2000, http://www.cedmagazine.com/ced/0010/104.htm.

72. Jeff Hecht, "Fiber Optics to the Home," *Technology Review*, March/April 2000, http://www.technologyreview.com/articles/hecht0300.asp.

73. Sarah L. Roberts-Witt, "The Future: Broadband's Next Trick May Be Fiber-Optic," *ZD Net*, January 19, 2001, http://www.zdnet.com/products/stories/reviews/0,4161,2671140,00.html.

74. Paul W. Shumate Jr., "The Broadest Broadband," *Scientific American*, October 1999. pp. 104–105.

75. Stephen C. Fehr, "D.C.'s High-Tech Highways Wreaking Havoc on Traffic," *Washington Post*, March 21, 1999, p. A19.

76. Duffy Hayes, "Are Overbuilders Keeping the Pace," *CED*, April 2002, http://www.rcn.com/investor/news/ced_mag.pdf.

77. http://www.rcn.com/.

78. Steve Twomey, "For Cable Customers, Competition Is Crucial: More Choices Leading to Faster, Better Service," *Washington Post*, May 23, 2002, p. D10.

79. Seth Schiesel, "Seizing the Phone Giants' Turf; Upstart RCN Digs in Despite Industry's Turmoil," *New York Times*, April 9, 2001, p. C1.

80. http://www.knology.com/.

81. http://www.wideopenwest.com/index.html. Also see Deborah Solomon, "WideOpenWest Issues a Challenge to Big Cable," *Wall Street Journal*, January 3, 2001, p. B4.

82. http://www.grandecom.com/index.jsp.

83. http://www.altrio.net/index1.asp?swf=0.

84. http://www.seren.com/.

85. Dennis Liebowitz and Karim Zia, "Overbuilders: Who Wants to Borrow a Billion?" *Media and Entertainment* 116 (Report from Donaldson, Lufkin & Jenrette) April 18, 2000, p. 7.

86. Neal Stephenson, "Mother Earth, Motherboard," *Wired*, December 1996, p. 97.

87. Mike Mills, "Undersea Cables Carry Growing Rivers of Data," *Washington Post*, March 9, 1998, p. A10.

88. Ibid.

89. Tom Geck, "Reload: Project Oxygen Takes a Deep Breath," *Red Herring*, March 2000, http://www.redherring.com/mag/issue76/mag-reloadpro-76.html.

90. Bryan Gruley, "Making Waves: Global Crossing Cries Foul as Carriers Opt for Rival Pacific Cable," *Wall Street Journal*, May 21, 1999, p. A1.

91. Ibid.

92. Gautam Naik, "Braving Sharks, Waves to Lay Phone Line," *Wall Street Journal*, September 12, 1997, p. B1.

93. Ibid.

94. Mills.

95. Rebecca Sausner, "Internet by Satellite: Will It Fly?" *NewsFactor Network*, May 2, 2001, www.newsfactor.com/perl/story/9412.html.

96. Peter S. Goodman, "Dishing Up a New Link to the Internet," *Washington Post*, November 6, 2000, p. A1; Phil Roosevelt, "A Heavenly Connection," *On Magazine*, April 2001, p. 68, http://www.onmagazine.com/on-mag/magazine/04012001/broadband_rev.html.

97. See Stephen Labaton, "An Earthly Idea for Doubling the Airwaves" *New York Times*, April 8, 2001, p. C1.

98. Peter S. Goodman, "McCaw Sets Sights Higher," *Washington Post*, April 24, 2001, p. E1.

99. Christine Y. Chen, "The Man Who Would Save Satellites," *Fortune*, July 8, 2002, pp. 101–108.

100. Reinhardt Krause, "Teledesic's Fall Could Free Radio Spectrum," *Investor's Business Daily*, October 9, 2002, p. A6.

101. See generally "Wounded Birds," *The Economist*, May 12, 2001, p. 68; and Lydia Lee, "Leader of the Space Race," *The Industry Standard*, November 27–December 4, 2000, pp. 100–104.

102. Adam Thierer and Clyde Wayne Crews Jr., "EchoStar-DirecTV Merger Critics Propose Infrastructure Socialism in Outer Space," Cato Institute *TechKnowledge* no. 41, October 8, 2002, http://www.cato.org/tech/tk/021008-tk.html.

103. Nancy Gohring, "Fixed Wireless Players Face Big Challenges," *Interactive Week*, July 2, 2001, p. 20.

104. Scott Woolley, "The Sky Is Calling," *Forbes*, May 13, 2002, pp. 151–54.

105. Wayne A. Leighton, "Broadband Deployment and the Digital Divide," Cato Institute Policy Analysis no. 410, August 7, 2001, http://www.cato.org/pubs/pas/pa-410es.html.

106. John Markoff, "2 Tinkerers Say They've Found a Cheap Way to Broadband," *New York Times*, June 10, 2002, p. C1.

107. See Brendan I. Koerner, "The Long Road to Internet Nirvana," *Wired*, October 2002, pp. 109–15; Nichols Negroponte, "Being Wireless," *Wired*, October 2002, pp. 116–19.

108. Paul Boutin, "Waiting for Wi-Fi," *Salon.com*, March 5, 2002, http://www.salon.com/tech/feature/2002/03/05/wi_fi_nation/?x.

109. John Markoff, "Talks Weigh Big Project on Wireless Internet Link," *New York Times*, July 16, 2002, p. C1.

110. Erick Schonfeld, "Unwiring the Masses," *Business 2.0*, June 2002, pp. 19–20.

111. http://www.boingo.com/.

112. http://www.hereuare.com/.

113. http://www.skypilot.com/.

114. http://www.wayport.com/.

115. http://www.ipass.com/main.php.

116. Roger O. Crockett, Heather Green, Andy Reinhardt, and Jay Greene, "All Net, All the Time," *Business Week*, April 29, 2002, p. 102.

117. Markoff.

118. Heather Green, "You Say You Want a Revolution?" *Business Week,* April 29, 2002, p. 108.

119. Ben Charny, "Cable Companies Cracking Down on Wi-Fi," *CNET News.com*, July 9, 2002, http://news.com.com/2100-1033-942323.html; and Patrick Ross, "Broadband," *Washington Internet Daily*, July 11, 2002, pp. 6–7.

120. Quentin Hardy, "The Great Wi-Fi Hope," *Forbes*, March 18, 2002, http://www.forbes.com/forbes/2002/0318/056_print.html.

121. Patrick Ross, "Wi-Fi Said to Solve Broadband Problem If Regulators Don't Block It," *Washington Internet Daily* 3, no. 120, pp. 1–2.

122. Matt Carolan, "Making Room for UWB," *EWeek*, February 25, 2002, p. 25.

123. "Watch This Airspace," *The Economist*, June 22, 2002, http://www.economist.com/printedition/displayStory.cfm?Story_ID=1176136.

124. Quoted in Yuki Noguchi, "Wireless Workhorse," *Washington Post*, July 6, 2002, p. E2.

125. John McCorkle, "Why Such Uproar over Ultrawideband?" *Communication Systems Design*, March 1, 2002, p. 31.

126. Federal Communications Commission, "In the Matter of Revision of Part 15 of the Commission's Rules Regarding Ultra-Wideband Transmission Systems," ET Docket No. 98-153, February 14, 2002, http://hraunfoss.fcc.gov/edocs_public/attachmatch/FCC-02-48A1.pdf.

127. http://www.xtremespectrum.com/.

128. http://www.timedomain.com/.

129. Corey Grice, "Science-Fiction Staple New Entry in High-Speed Net," *CNET News.com*, March 22, 2000, http://news.com.com/2100-1033-238249.html?legacy=cnet; Anne Eisenberg, "No Fiber Optic Link? Try a Leapfrogging Laser Beam," *New*

*York Times,* February 7, 2002, p. E9; Byron Acohido, "Free-Space Optics Offer Fast Data with Fewer Physical Links; FSO's Lasers Lessen Need to Directly Tap Fiber-Optic Lines," *USA Today,* April 11, 2002. p. 1B.

130. http://www.terabeam.com/.

131. http://www.airfiber.com/index.shtml.

132. http://www.lightpointe.com/.

133. James Hattori, "Terabeam Aims to Solve 'Last Mile' Data Jam," *CNN.com,* February 27, 2001, http://www.cnn.com/2001/TECH/internet/02/27/terabeam/.

134. Grice.

135. Brian E. Taptich, "Laser Beams Focus on Broadband," *Red Herring,* March 2002, p. 78.

136. Ibid.

137. Peter S. Goodman, "Rooftops Loom as a Telecom Battleground," *Washington Post,* June 12, 2000, p. A1, http://www.washingtonpost.com/ac2/wp-dyn?pagename = article&node = &contentId = A29372-2000Jun9; Derrick Cain, "Constitutional Issues Arise in Debate about Forced Access for Wireless," *BNA Daily Report for Executives,* March 22, 2000, p. A-20.

138. Adam Thierer, "The FCC's Bizarre Building Mandate," *Tech Central Station.com,* October 2, 2000, http://www.techcentralstation.com/1051/techwrapper. jsp?PID = 1051-250&CID = 1051-100200H.

139. Anthony Acampora, "Last Mile by Laser," *Scientific American.com,* June 17, 2002, http://www.sciam.com/article.cfm?articleID = 0008069E-808A-1D06-8E49809 EC588EEDF&catID = 2.

## Chapter 7

1. For the most comprehensive overview of retransmission consent law and regulation, see Charles Lubinsky, "Reconsidering Retransmission Consent: An Examination of the Retransmission Consent Provision" [47 U.S.C. 325 (b)] of the 1992 Cable Act," *Federal Communications Law Journal* 49, no. 1 (November 1996): 99–165, http://www.law.indiana.edu/fclj/pubs/v49/no1/lubinsky.html.

2. See *Fortnightly Corporation v. United Artists Television, Inc.,* 392 U.S. 390 (1968); and *Teleprompter Corp. v. Columbia Broadcasting Systems, Inc.* 415 U.S. 394 (1974).

3. *Quincy Cable TV, Inc. v. FCC,* 768 F. 2d 1434 (D.C. Circuit, 1985).

4. *Century Communications Corp. v. FCC,* 835 F. 2d 292 (D.C. Circuit, 1987).

5. *Turner Broadcasting System, Inc. v. FCC,* 512 U.S. 622 (1994).

6. See Pilon, pp. 41–63.

7. *Turner Broadcasting System, Inc v. FCC,* 520 U.S. 180 (1997).

8. Federal Communications Commission, "Notice of Proposed Rulemaking in the Matter of Carriage of Digital Television Broadcast Signals," CS Docket 98-120, July 1998.

9. Adam Thierer, "The HDTV Fiasco Gets Worse: TV Set and Cable Mandates on the Way," Cato Institute *TechKnowledge* no. 39, August 5, 2002.

10. For more information, see Thomas W. Hazlett, "The U.S. Digital TV Transition: Time to Toss the Negroponte Switch," AEI-Brookings Joint Center for Regulatory Studies, Working Paper no. 01-15, November 2001.

11. Thomas W. Hazlett, "Heavy Burden," *Forbes ASAP,* November 27, 2000, p. 270, http://www.forbes.com/asap/2000/1127/270.html.

12. "Because of the natural advantage in local markets enjoyed by local stations over stations originating elsewhere, only local stations that are particularly inept at devising programming to meet viewer demands are in need of such protection." Donald J. Boudreaux and Robert B. Ekelund, Jr., "Cable Reregulation," *Cato Journal* 14, no. 1 (Spring/Summer 1994): 98.

13. Peter Huber, *Law and Disorder in Cyberspace: Abolish the FCC and Let Common Law Rule the Telecosm* (New York: Oxford University Press, 1997), p. 149.

14. Thomas W. Hazlett, "Digitizing 'Must-Carry' Under *Turner Broadcasting v. FCC,*" *Supreme Court Economic Review* 8 (2000): 154, http://www.manhattan-institute.org/hazlett/rahazl1.pdf.

15. Federal Communications Commission, "In the Matter of Implementation of the Satellite Home Viewer Improvement Act of 1999," CS Docket No. 99-363, March 16, 2000, http://www.fcc.gov/Bureaus/Cable/Orders/2000/fcc00099.pdf

16. See Adam D. Thierer and Bryan T. Johnson, "Why Congress Must Fix the Satellite Home Viewer Act," Heritage Foundation Backgrounder no. 1254, February 19, 1999, http://www.heritage.org/library/backgrounder/bg1254.html.

17. Brody Mullins, "Satellite TV Firms Offer Service Pledge to Coax Merger," *National Journal's Congress Daily AM*, March 6, 2002.

## Chapter 8

1. Noted in Ariana Eunjung Cha and Dina ElBoghdady, "Industry Looks for Signs," *Washington Post*, September 7, 2001, http://www.washtech.com/news/software/12365-1.html.

2. "Schumer Says He Is Abandoning His Support for Microsoft," *National Journal's Congress Daily*, July 24, 2001.

3. "Trying to Connect You," *The Economist*, June 24, 2000, p. 69.

4. See Jim Hu, "Gates Urges Regulators to Address Instant Messaging," *CNET News.com*, December 18, 2000, http://news.com.com/2100-1023-250008.html?legacy=cnet.

5. For example, see Lisa M. Bowman, "AOL Shuts Out Users in Battle over IM," *ZDNet News*, January 30, 2002, http://zdnet.com.com/2100-1105-826707.html.

6. OMNI is available at www.emphatech.com.

7. Thomas E. Weber, "Here's Instant Message for Chat Technology: Time 4 U to Grow Up," *Wall Street Journal*, February 25, 2002, p. B1.

8. Gasman, p. 40.

## Chapter 9

1. Douglas Houston, "The Case for Deregulating Electric Transmission: The Virtues of Self-Governance," Paper prepared for the Cato Institute/Institute for Energy Research Conference on New Horizons in Electric Power Deregulation, Renaissance Hotel, Washington, D.C., March 2, 1995, p. 12.

# Index

# About the Authors

### Clyde Wayne Crews Jr.

Clyde Wayne Crews Jr. is the director of technology studies at the Cato Institute where he studies Internet and technology regulation, antitrust, and other regulatory reforms. Earlier, Crews was director of competition and regulation policy at the Competitive Enterprise Institute, and a legislative aide to Sen. Phil Gramm (R-Tex.), responsible for regulatory and welfare reform issues. He has been an economist and policy analyst at the Citizens for a Sound Economy Foundation, and has worked as an economist at the Food and Drug Administration and a research assistant at the Center for the Study of Public Choice at George Mason University. Crews has published in the *Wall Street Journal, Forbes*, the *Washington Times*, the *Journal of Commerce, American Enterprise, Policy Sciences*, the *Electricity Journal*, and others. He has appeared on various television and radio programs including CNN, Fox News, Tech TV, TechnoPolitics, PBS, and others.

### Adam Thierer

Adam Thierer is the director of telecommunications studies at the Cato Institute where he conducts research on how government regulations are hampering the evolution of communications networks, including telephony, broadcasting, cable, satellite, and the Internet. He also examines the broader economic and constitutional aspects of telecommunications policy. His writing has been published in the *Washington Post, Newsweek, Wall Street Journal, Investors Business Daily, Journal of Commerce, Forbes*, and *The Economist*. He has made media appearances on NPR, PBS, Fox News Channel, CNN, MSNBC, BBC, Radio Free Europe, and Voice of America. Prior to joining Cato, Thierer spent nine years at the Heritage Foundation, where he served as the Alex C. Walker Fellow in Economic Policy. In that capacity, he covered telecommunications and Internet policy and also wrote extensively on antitrust, electricity and energy policy, the airline industry, and federalism. Before moving to Washington, Thierer worked at the Adam Smith Institute in London, England, where he examined reform of the British legal system.

# Cato Institute

Founded in 1977, the Cato Institute is a public policy research foundation dedicated to broadening the parameters of policy debate to allow consideration of more options that are consistent with the traditional American principles of limited government, individual liberty, and peace. To that end, the Institute strives to achieve greater involvement of the intelligent, concerned lay public in questions of policy and the proper role of government.

The Institute is named for *Cato's Letters*, libertarian pamphlets that were widely read in the American Colonies in the early 18th century and played a major role in laying the philosophical foundation for the American Revolution.

Despite the achievement of the nation's Founders, today virtually no aspect of life is free from government encroachment. A pervasive intolerance for individual rights is shown by government's arbitrary intrusions into private economic transactions and its disregard for civil liberties.

To counter that trend, the Cato Institute undertakes an extensive publications program that addresses the complete spectrum of policy issues. Books, monographs, and shorter studies are commissioned to examine the federal budget, Social Security, regulation, military spending, international trade, and myriad other issues. Major policy conferences are held throughout the year, from which papers are published thrice yearly in the *Cato Journal*. The Institute also publishes the quarterly magazine *Regulation*.

In order to maintain its independence, the Cato Institute accepts no government funding. Contributions are received from foundations, corporations, and individuals, and other revenue is generated from the sale of publications. The Institute is a nonprofit, tax-exempt, educational foundation under Section 501(c)3 of the Internal Revenue Code.

CATO INSTITUTE
1000 Massachusetts Ave., N.W.
Washington, D.C. 20001